Planting by Numbers

hamlyn

Planting by Numbers

Tim Newbury

First published in Great Britain in 2002 by
Hamlyn, a division of Octopus Publishing Group Ltd
2–4 Heron Quays, London E14 4JP

ISBN 0 600 60320 2

A CIP catalogue record for this book is available from the British Library

Printed and bound in China

10 9 8 7 6 5 4 3 2 1

Contents

Introduction 6
How to Use this Book 7

Beds and Borders 8

Rectangular Borders 10
Evergreen Rectangular Border 12
Exotic Rectangular Border 14
Traditional Herbaceous Border 16
Long, Narrow Borders 18
Cottage-garden Border 20
Long, Narrow Border for Wildlife 22
Single-colour Border 24
Island Beds 26
Flower Arranger's Island Bed 28
Foliage Island Bed 30
Single-colour Island Bed 32
Corner Beds 34
Mediterranean Corner Bed 36
Moist, Shady Corner Bed 38
Corner Bed for Wildlife 40
Raised Beds 42
Raised Bed with Year-round Interest 44
Low-maintenance Raised Bed 46
Colour-themed Raised Bed 48
Formal Beds 50
Formal Foliage Bed 52
Formal Colour Theme 54
Formal Garden in Shade 56
Kitchen Gardens 58
Culinary Herb Garden 60
Ornamental Herb Garden 62
Vegetable Garden 64

Garden Designs 66

Small Front Gardens 68
Low-maintenance Front Garden 70
Foliage Front Garden 72
Cottage-garden-style Front Garden 74
Sloping Gardens 76
Hot, Dry Sloping Garden 78
Sloping Garden with 'Cool' Colour Scheme 80
Sloping Terrace Garden in Shade 82
Patio Gardens 84
Gravel Patio Garden 86
Colour-themed Patio Garden 88
Patio with Year-round Interest 90
Courtyard Gardens 92
Cottage-garden-style Courtyard 94
Shady Courtyard Garden 96
Minimalist Courtyard Garden 98

Container Gardening 100

Containers 102
Containers for Summer Colour 104
Year-round Container Planting 106
Foliage Plants in Containers 108
Windowboxes and Wall Baskets 110
Planting for Spring 112
Summer Bedding 114
Winter Colour 116
Balconies and Roof Gardens 118
Hot, Dry Roof Garden 120
Shady Roof Garden 122
Year-round Roof Garden 124

Index 126
Acknowledgements 128

Introduction

Choosing a planting scheme for a new garden or part of an existing garden can be a daunting prospect. Not only is there the difficulty of choosing suitable plants from among the thousands that are now available, but you must also decide on the type of garden you want: formal or informal, traditional or modern, a garden filled with vivid colours or somewhere calming to relax after a busy day at work, a garden that is easy to look after or one that will require constant attention. The choice of hard landscaping materials for patios, paths and walls is also vital, because these are likely to outlast many of the plants.

This book has been planned to aid the decision-making process and to help you assess the features – new and existing – that will affect your choice of garden design. It covers all the main garden types, from informal borders to formal plots, from corner beds to small front gardens, from patio gardens to windowboxes. There is also advice on planting herbs and vegetables so that even a small area can be used to provide fresh produce for the kitchen. No matter how large or small your own space, you will find a design here that can be readily adapted to suit the conditions you have in your own garden.

Alternative planting schemes are suggested for many of the designs, to cater for differing garden conditions or for varying preferences with regard to colour. Schemes that are based on the calming and cooling shades of blue, white and yellow, for example, may not be to your taste, but simply replacing some of the key plants with bolder or more dramatically coloured foliage or flowers will completely change the atmosphere of your garden.

No matter how large or small your garden, you will find in these pages ideas for beds and borders that can be used in your own garden or adapted to suit your own circumstances and desires.

How to Use this Book

Each section consists of four double-page spreads, the first of which provides an introduction to the topic, for example rectangular borders. The following three spreads, options 1–3, are each dedicated to a specific planting design for exactly the same area.

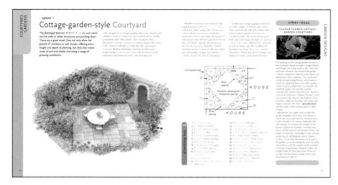

Options 1 and 2

Option 3

Options 1 and 2

On these spreads, you will find a full-colour illustration of the finished planting design, together with a description of the main attributes of the chosen plants and how they combine within the design. There is a detailed overhead plan of the area, showing exactly which plant should be planted in each position. In addition, there is a panel giving either a description of how to adapt the planting design to create a different effect or to adapt it to a different situation ('other ideas'), or a detailed profile of a plant group, such as ferns, or a particular 'feature' plant.

Option 3

On this spread, the same elements are present as for options 1 and 2, except for the illustration of the finished design, which is replaced by a panel giving extra information regarding a particlar aspect of this third design option, such as planting perennials or creating a focal point.

Beds and Borders

Most gardens, large or small, include beds or borders, where colourful annuals, reliable shrubs and perennials and stately trees can be grown for year-round interest. Successful planting is not just a question of choosing plants that look good together, however; it is also important to select plants that will grow well together in the same kind of conditions.

Rectangular Borders

If there is space in your garden, having deep beds and borders against a boundary wall or fence can be an advantage because they allow you to grow taller, larger plants towards the back, which will enhance the sense of scale and improve the overall effect of the planting as well as allowing you to screen unsightly objects beyond, such as the top of an old shed in your neighbour's garden or a view of a distant pylon.

The rectangular bed illustrated overleaf could be considered as an island bed that has been divided in two by the fence, leaving half the bed on your side. A general rule in island beds is not to have plants that are taller than about half the depth of the bed – in this case about 3m (10ft). For narrower beds you should reduce the maximum height of the plants accordingly.

The shape of this bed is deliberately emphasized by the use of slate paving around three sides, and this has the bonus of providing a mowing strip that makes grass-cutting simpler. The boundary behind the bed is a wooden panel fence, with the boards of each panel fixed in a diagonal or 'chevron' pattern, and round ball finials on top of each post as a finishing touch. The strong, horizontal line of the top of the fence is deliberately interrupted by the taller planting at the back of the border, and the geometric chevron pattern of the dark grey boards is a striking contrast to the flowers and foliage in front.

• option 1

Evergreen Rectangular Border

This easy-care border, planted entirely with evergreens, provides a surprising amount of seasonal interest in terms of changes in foliage colour and flowering periods.

Male flowers of the variegated holly *Ilex aquifolium* 'Handsworth New Silver' are essential to pollinate the female flowers of *I. aquifolium* 'Alaska' nearby and produce masses of bright red winter berries. At the back of the bed, on the fence, is *Clematis armandii*, which bears masses of beautiful, sweetly scented cream and yellow flowers in early spring. Soon afterwards, the bold, glossy green leaves of *Rhododendron* 'Mother of Pearl' provide a perfect foil to the large heads of deep lilac-pink, trumpet-shaped flowers, which contrast with the slender, upright, greenish-yellow stems and soft

green, grassy leaves of bamboo *Fargesia murieliae* 'Simba'. The startling red new growths of *Pieris formosa* var. *forrestii* 'Wakehurst' are followed by hanging clusters of tiny, white bell-flowers. Flowering interest lasts all summer: the pink papery 'roses' of *Cistus* 'Silver Pink', the long succession of pinkish-white, tubular blooms and golden-tinged foliage of *Abelia* × *grandiflora* 'Francis Mason' and the dense white spikes and bright

golden foliage of the late-summer heather *Calluna vulgaris* 'Gold Haze'.

Contrasts in foliage form and colour abound, with the purple-tinged swords of *Phormium tenax* Purpureum Group and the low, grassy mounds of *Liriope muscari* (lilyturf), which produces purple berry-like flowers in autumn. These stand out against the neat, pale green mound of *Hebe* 'White Gem'; it has a profusion of small white flower spikes in early summer.

other ideas

DRY, ALKALINE GARDENS

The evergreen plants in this rectangular border do well in a reasonably good, slightly acid soil. However, on drier, neutral or slightly alkaline soils, some of them will do less well, and you will need to make a few changes. Ericaceous plants – that is, those needing an acid soil – will not thrive, which means replacing the rhododendron, pieris and calluna. Instead you might put the flowering currant *Ribes viburnifolium*, *Photinia fraseri* 'Rubens', which has startlingly red new growth, and *Euonymus fortunei* 'Emerald 'n' Gold', which will provide a splash of colour low down. Another alternative for the calluna would be the dwarf holly *Ilex crenata* 'Golden Gem'. In addition, you might plant a *Cordyline australis* 'Atropurpurea' instead of the phormium and replace the fargesia with another bamboo, such as *Sasa tsuboiana*.

The clematis on the fence prefers good, moisture-retentive soil, so you might need to introduce a different evergreen climber here, such as the silver, grey and green ivy *Hedera colchica* 'Dentata Variegata'. At the front of the border is *Acorus gramineus* 'Ogon', which is sometimes used as a pond marginal, so in dry soil it is best replaced by the neat golden tufts of *Festuca glauca* 'Golden Toupee'. *Helleborus argutifolius* (Corsican hellebore) will tolerate some dryness if it is not planted in direct sun, but in a hot, sunny position you would be better to use a foliage plant that is more tolerant of drought, such as *Ballota pseudodictamnus* (**pictured above**).

Chevron screen fence

Slate paving

L A W N

planting key

1 *Clematis armandii*
2 *Ilex aquifolium* 'Handsworth New Silver'
3 *Rhododendron* 'Mother of Pearl'
4 *Ilex aquifolium* 'Alaska'
5 *Elaeagnus pungens* 'Maculata'
6 *Cistus* 'Silver Pink'
7 *Pieris formosa* var. *forrestii* 'Wakehurst'
8 *Fargesia murieliae* 'Simba'
9 *Phormium tenax* Purpureum Group
10 *Abelia* × *grandiflora* 'Francis Mason'
11 *Erica vagans* 'Mrs D.F. Maxwell'
12 *Helleborus argutifolius*
13 *Hebe* 'Great Orme'
14 *Sarcococca hookeriana* var. *digyna*
15 *Calluna vulgaris* 'Gold Haze'
16 *Bergenia* 'Sunningdale'
17 *Hebe* 'White Gem'
18 *Helianthemum* 'Rhodanthe Carneum'
19 *Acorus gramineus* 'Ogon'
20 *Erica carnea* 'King George'
21 *Liriope muscari*

• option 2

Exotic Rectangular Border

The exotic appearance of the blooms and leaves in this version of a rectangular border belies the fact that most, if not all, of the plants are relatively hardy, and certainly do not require a subtropical climate in order to do well.

One of the most eye-catching plants in this border is the stiff-stemmed climber *Campsis* x *tagliabuana*

'Madame Galen', which, if planted in a warm, sheltered position, produces huge, bright orange trumpets in late summer over glossy green leaflets. The large *Abutilon vitifolium* needs a similar situation for its soft, vine-like leaves and saucer-shaped, mauve flowers, borne right through from late spring to midsummer.

Next to these, the dark purple foliage of the hardy hazel *Corylus maxima* 'Purpurea' makes a dramatic

contrast and also forms a striking backdrop to the fragrant, white trumpets of *Lilium candidum* (Madonna lily). Equally striking in flower is the hardy arum, *Zantedeschia aethiopica* 'Crowborough', which has huge, white flower spathes arising from clumps of lush green foliage in a moist situation. Similar conditions suit the perennial *Roscoea cautleyoides* 'Kew Beauty', with leafy stems and a succession of beautiful primrose-yellow flowers, which look like orchids. Dramatic foliage is also in evidence throughout the bed in the huge, spiky variegated leaflets of *Aralia elata* 'Variegata', the blue-green, pinnate foliage and stiff upright stems of *Decaisnea fargesii*, with its amazing blue 'bean' pods, and at the back the tall stems and long, arching leaves of *Arundo donax* (giant reed), which sway and rustle in the wind.

plant focus

SHRUBS

Shrubs are the backbone of many gardens: a permanent framework of branches and leaves, mixed with periods of flower and fruit. Given space and in the right conditions, some shrubs, like the purple-leaved hazel *Corylus maxima* 'Purpurea', can achieve almost tree-like size, while tiny cultivars, such as *Berberis thunbergii* 'Bagatelle' and *Hebe pinguifolia* 'Pagei', are just as happy in a windowbox as in a large border.

Shrubs flower in all seasons – the fragrant white flowers of *Viburnum farreri* and the scented yellow spikes of *Mahonia* × *media* 'Winter Sun' (**pictured above**) appear in late autumn and winter. Flowers of all shapes, colours and sizes range from the massive blue heads of *Hydrangea macrophylla* 'Mariesii Perfecta' to the tiny white stars of *Hebe armstrongii*. Variations in foliage are just as dramatic, from red new growth of *Photinia* × *fraseri* 'Red Robin' to the huge sculptural leaves of *Aralia elata* and *Mahonia lomariifolia*.

Sun-loving cistus and lavenders do well on dry soil, while azaleas and rhododendrons prefer cooler, acid soil in light shade. For heavy shade look out for *Prunus laurocerasus* (cherry laurel, laurel) and *Ilex* species (holly). *Salix* species (willow) and *Cornus* species (dogwood) thrive in moist conditions. Many shrubs are valued for their long or varied season – *Viburnum opulus* 'Compactum', for example, has white lacecap flowers in spring followed by clusters of shiny orange-red berries for brilliant autumn colour.

Chevron screen fence

Slate paving

L A W N

planting key

1 *Campsis* × *tagliabuana* 'Madame Galen'
2 *Crinodendron hookerianum*
3 *Arundo donax*
4 *Abutilon vitifolium*
5 *Corylus maxima* 'Purpurea'
6 *Lilium candidum*
7 *Acca sellowiana*
8 *Aralia elata* 'Variegata'
9 *Decaisnea fargesii*
10 *Euphorbia griffithii* 'Fireglow'
11 *Zantedeschia aethiopica* 'Crowborough'
12 *Phormium* 'Sundowner'
13 *Asphodeline lutea*
14 *Phygelius rectus* 'African Queen'
15 *Iris* 'Dancers Veil'
16 *Platycodon grandiflorus*
17 *Imperata cylindrica* 'Red Baron'
18 *Penstemon newberryi*
19 *Allium schubertii*
20 *Roscoea cautleyoides* 'Kew Beauty'
21 *Agapanthus* 'Lilliput'

• option 3

Traditional Herbaceous Border

The partly island-bed nature of this border makes it possible to grow tall perennials at the back, grading down to lower, more compact forms near the front; in the process you will achieve a substantial feature.

As a backdrop, the strong-growing climber *Rosa* 'Albertine' has a succession of scented, copper-pink flowers and glossy foliage. The brown-centred, gold stars of the coneflower *Rudbeckia* 'Juligold' and the tall pink spikes of *Alcea rosea* (hollyhock) provide both late flowers and height. The tall *Thalictrum flavum* subsp. *glaucum* has subtle sulphur-yellow flowerheads above glaucous foliage. *Kniphofia uvaria* (red-hot poker) is invaluable for its clumps of narrow leaves and bold spikes of long-lasting red and yellow flowers, which contrast with the elegant white saucers of *Anemone* × *hybrida* 'Honorine Jobert'. Perennials that extend the season include *Crocosmia* × *crocosmiiflora* 'Emily McKenzie', with burnt-orange flowers in late summer, *Campanula persicifolia* with its summer-long blue bells,

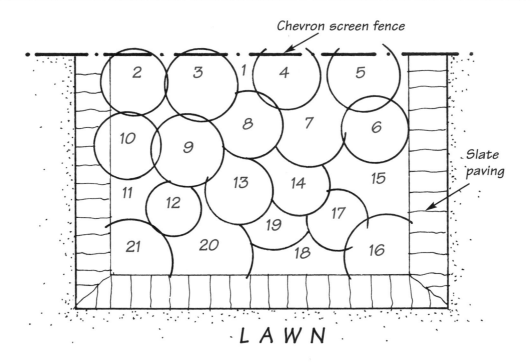

Chevron screen fence

Slate paving

L A W N

planting key

1 *Rosa* 'Albertine'
2 *Aruncus dioicus*
3 *Rudbeckia* 'Juligold'
4 *Alcea rosea* (salmon-pink form)
5 *Thalictrum flavum* subsp. *glaucum*
6 *Kniphofia uvaria*
7 *Ligularia* 'The Rocket'
8 *Delphinium* Black Knight Group
9 *Anemone* × *hybrida* 'Honorine Jobert'
10 *Euphorbia wallichii*
11 *Artemisia* 'Powis Castle'
12 *Crocosmia* × *crocosmiiflora* 'Emily McKenzie'
13 *Phlox maculata* 'Omega'
14 *Astilbe* × *arendsii* 'Bressingham Beauty'
15 *Campanula persicifolia*
16 *Sedum* 'Herbstfreude'
17 *Tradescantia andersoniana* 'Purewell Giant'
18 *Primula denticulata*
19 *Salvia nemorosa* 'Ostfriesland'
20 *Solidago* 'Queenie'
21 *Geranium sanguineum*

and *Euphorbia wallichii*, with its narrow silver-veined leaves and pale yellow flowers and bracts in early summer.

Foliage interest is equally important. The large, jagged leaves of *Ligularia* 'The Rocket' and its tall, black-stemmed spikes of yellow flowers contrast with the finely cut, glossy green foliage and shell-pink flower plumes of *Astilbe* × *arendsii* 'Bressingham Beauty'. The soft, silver-grey, pungent mound of *Artemisia* 'Powis Castle' provides a link and foil for the euphorbia, crocosmia and the smaller but long-flowering *Geranium sanguineum*, with its deep magenta, saucer-shaped flowers produced from early summer.

Sedum 'Herbstfreude' is an excellent late summer flowering perennial, particularly valuable for beneficial insects such as bees, butterflies and hoverflies.

Planting Perennials

In a small border with enough room for 10–15 perennials, it is perfectly acceptable to use an individual plant of each of 10–15 varieties for it to look full and balanced. However, in a larger border, where there might be space for maybe five or six times this number of plants, using a single plant of 60 or 70 varieties would result in a busy, unsatisfying mixture.

In these larger areas you should plant perennials in groups of three, five or even more of the same kind, so that the impact of each is greater. This will partly depend on the vigour and habit of the individual plant. For example, a mature single plant of the large-leaved *Ligularia dentata* 'Desdemona' (**pictured right**) may reach as much as 75–90cm (30–36in) across, whereas a single geranium may not exceed half that size. Thus, for a group of three ligularias, you would need to plant seven or nine geraniums to achieve a visual balance. Always use odd numbers of plants – if you use even numbers it is too easy to end up with a square

or linear group that looks stiff and unnatural.

Although it is tempting to pack perennials closer together than their ultimate spread for quick and effective cover, the overcrowding can cause leaf and flower stems to become weak and drawn as they compete for light. This makes them not only floppy but also more susceptible to pests and diseases.

other ideas

PROVIDING YEAR-ROUND INTEREST

Traditional herbaceous borders tend to have a main season of interest from spring to autumn, usually peaking over the summer months, but with little structure or interest in the depths of winter. This is not a problem if the border is part of a larger garden where there are other areas of attraction in winter. In small gardens, however, you may need to supplement the herbaceous perennials with shrubs to provide the missing winter interest, thereby making it more of a mixed border.

You could begin on the screen fence by adding an evergreen climber or two, such as *Clematis cirrhosa* var. *balearica*, which has the bonus of winter flowers, or the bright gold-splashed *Hedera colchica* 'Sulphur Heart'. Winter-flowering shrubs, such as the pink, scented *Viburnum* × *bodnantense* 'Dawn' and the yellow, spidery flowers of *Hamamelis* × *intermedia* 'Pallida', could be used to replace the tall perennials – the aruncus, rudbeckia, hollyhock and thalictrum (meadow rue) – at the back of the border. Nearer the front the grey-leaved artemisia could be replaced by the similarly coloured *Hebe* 'Red Edge', which has white flowers in summer and red winter tints. You could also use *Geranium macrorrhizum* 'Ingwersen's Variety' in place of *G. sanguineum*, for its evergreen foliage, again with good tints in cold weather.

Long, Narrow Borders

One of the keys to a successful garden, particularly those of a modest size, is to try to hide or disguise the boundaries, especially where they are straight and rigid. Well-grown climbers, supported by horizontal wires, or trellis panels attached to fences and walls can be effective in achieving this. Sometimes, however, this is not always entirely successful, because the chosen climber cannot grow higher than the structure and will cling quite tightly to it, creating in time what is really a climber 'hedge' that, although green and flowering, will still be straight and level. Moreover, the boundary might be a rather attractive old brick or natural stone wall, and it would be shame to mask it completely.

An attractive solution would be to create a relatively long, narrow border, such as the one illustrated overleaf. Be careful to make the edge a combination of long, sweeping curves in order to draw the eye away from any straight lines. Climbers used on the wall behind have been carefully chosen to break up, but not completely hide, the brickwork, which can then act as a foil or backdrop to the plants in front of it.

Within the border itself the planting has been largely graded, with the lowest species at the front and ends and the tallest at the back. Taller plants with an upright or narrow habit are of particular value because they do not take up as much room on the ground and their height helps to break up the horizontal line of the wall coping behind.

• option 1

Cottage-garden Border

This design for a long, narrow border consists of a traditional mix of perennials to create a stunning old-fashioned cottage-garden effect, and is very easy to maintain. All of these plants have been selected for their form and colour, and because they are both reliable and healthy. In addition, none of them will require staking.

It is a border for summer-long interest, starting to become attractive in late spring with the brilliant yellow of the neat, low *Euphorbia polychroma* and the bold blue and white flags and sword-shaped foliage of the tall bearded *Iris* 'Braithwaite', and not finishing until well into the autumn with the bright pink, daisy-like flowers of *Aster amellus* 'Brilliant'. Between these is a succession of summer flowers and foliage: the blue bells of

Campanula lactiflora, the large, white, shaggy heads of *Leucanthemum superbum* 'Alaska' and the beautiful shell pink, fluffy sprays of the dwarf *Astilbe* 'Sprite'.

Foliage variations are just as important in this type of bed. The soft, fine grey of *Artemisia* 'Powis Castle' is a lovely contrast to the green, spiky leaves and burnt orange-red flowers of *Crocosmia* 'Emberglow', and the bold glaucous and beige leaves of *Hosta* 'Frances Williams'

gleam next to the delicate pink flowerheads of *Scabiosa* 'Pink Mist'.

Variation in height at the back breaks up the line of the wall. The tall yellow spikes of *Verbascum* 'Gainsborough', the dark blue bells of *Delphinium* Black Knight Group and the beautiful gold, hazy seedheads of *Stipa gigantea* (giant feather grass, golden oats) all tower above the basal clumps of slender, grey-green leaves.

Brick Wall **Stone pier caps**

25 24 23

22 19 18 16 14 12 10 8 6 2 1
21 20 17 15 13 11 9 7 4 5 3

L A W N

planting key

1 *Aster amellus* 'Brilliant'
2 *Campanula lactiflora*
3 *Euphorbia polychroma*
4 *Leucanthemum superbum* 'Alaska'
5 *Geranium clarkei* 'Kashmir Purple'
6 *Lysimachia ciliata* 'Firecracker'
7 *Scabiosa* 'Pink Mist'
8 *Iris* 'Braithwaite'
9 *Hosta* 'Frances Williams'
10 *Verbascum* 'Gainsborough'
11 *Artemisia* 'Powis Castle'
12 *Crocosmia* 'Emberglow'
13 *Sedum aizooon* 'Euphorbioides'

14 *Phlox paniculata* 'Sandringham'
15 *Salvia sylvestris* 'Blauhügel'
16 *Lupinus* 'Noble Maiden'
17 *Pulmonaria saccharata* Argentea Group
18 *Rudbeckia* 'Goldquelle'
19 *Stipa gigantea*
20 *Astilbe* 'Sprite'
21 *Dianthus* 'Devon Maid'
22 *Delphinium* Black Knight Group
23 *Rosa* 'Albertine'
24 *Lonicera periclymenum* 'Belgica'
25 *Clematis* 'Vyvyan Pennell'

other ideas

COTTAGE GARDEN IN SHADE

Long, narrow borders are often backed with a solid barrier – wall, fence or hedge – and these barriers frequently cast a shadow over the border for much of the day. Many plants thrive in these conditions, including the campanula, euphorbia, hosta and *Lonicera periclymenum* 'Belgica' (early Dutch honeysuckle).

Other plants will not achieve their full potential in these conditions and need more direct sunlight. Replace any soft, grey-leaved plants, such as the verbascum, artemisia and *Stipa gigantea* (giant feather grass, golden oats), with more appropriate ones, such as *Digitalis* species (foxglove), another hosta, perhaps *H.* 'Halcyon', and the grass *Calamagrostis acutiflora* 'Overdam'. The honeysuckle and clematis on the fence are fine, but replace the rambling rose, *Rosa* 'Albertine', with *Clematis* 'Nelly Moser' (**pictured above**), or the less dramatic but sweetly scented flowers of *Akebia quinata*.

Dianthus cultivars are happiest in full sun, so replace *D.* 'Devon Maid' with the purple-red *Viola* 'Red Charm' or the taller, grassy-leaved *Tradescantia andersoniana* 'Pauline'. Asters and scabious also prefer sun; good alternatives for these plants are *Anemone* x *hybrida* 'Richard Ahrens', which produces pink flowers over a long period, and the shorter *Geranium macrorrhizum* 'Ingwersen's Variety', with rose-pink flowers and soft, dense, aromatic foliage.

• option 2

Long, Narrow Border for Wildlife

This border, with its mix of attractive flowers, foliage and seedheads, has been designed to be especially interesting to smaller creatures, such as insects.

Encouraging insect life into gardens is desirable for several reasons. First, some insects – ladybirds and lacewings, for example – prey on other insects that are usually thought of as pests, such as aphids. Second, they themselves are food for larger creatures, particularly birds like wrens and blue tits. Finally, bees, hoverflies and other flying insects transfer pollen around the garden, helping to pollinate fruiting and seeding plants.

There is great variation in the bed. Evergreens, such as the neat mound and masses of sky-blue flower spikes

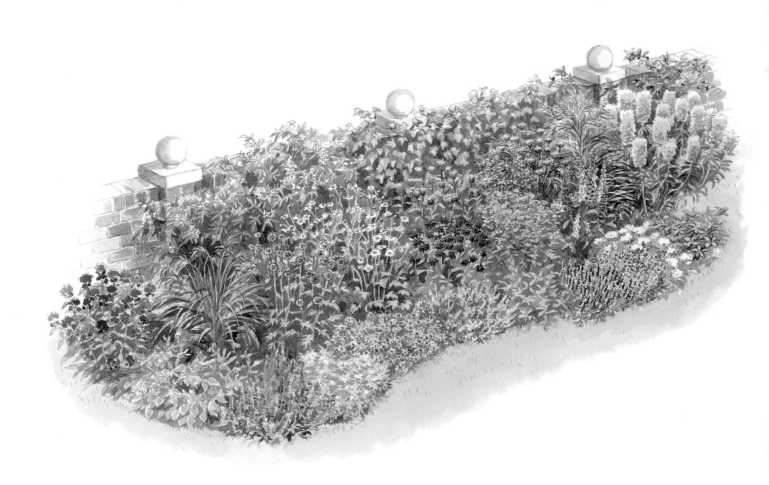

of *Hebe* 'Margret', and the bold, gold-splashed leaves of the ivy *Hedera colchica* 'Sulphur Heart', grow alongside the dark leaves and heavily scented flowers of *Lonicera henryi* (honeysuckle). The jagged silver-green leaves of *Eryngium agavifolium* (sea holly), with its blue, thistle-like heads, contrast strongly with the soft bronze-green haze of *Foeniculum vulgare* 'Giant Bronze' (bronze fennel). Height is given by the upright spikes of

Digitalis purpurea Excelsior Group (foxglove) and the stout, dramatic foliage and bright yellow flowers of *Centaurea macrocephala* (knapweed). Particularly valuable are the long-flowering white-flowered *Sedum spectabile* 'Iceberg' (ice plant), the almost non-stop pink and red pokers of the groundcovering *Persicaria affinis* 'Donald Lowndes' and the equally floriferous *Centranthus ruber* var. *coccineus* (valerian), with its red flower clusters.

Brick wall Stone pier caps

L A W N

1 *Euphorbia characias* subsp. *wulfenii*
2 *Digitalis purpurea* Excelsior Group
3 *Skimmia japonica* 'Rubella'
4 *Miscanthus sinensis* 'Kleine Fontane'
5 *Sedum spectabile* 'Iceberg'
6 *Foeniculum vulgare* 'Giant Bronze'
7 *Hebe pimeleoides* 'Quicksilver'
8 *Eryngium agavifolium*
9 *Persicaria affinis* 'Donald Lowndes'
10 *Aster novae-angliae* 'Harrington's Pink'
11 *Skimmia japonica* 'Bowles' Dwarf Female'
12 *Centaurea macrocephala*
13 *Hebe* 'Margret'
14 *Monarda* 'Cambridge Scarlet'
15 *Coreopsis verticillata* 'Moonbeam'
16 *Anemone* × *hybrida* 'Honorine Jobert'
17 *Origanum vulgare* 'Thumble's Variety'
18 *Echinops ritro* 'Veitch's Blue'
19 *Stipa calamagrostis*
20 *Nepeta* × *faassenii*
21 *Symphytum* 'Goldsmith'
22 *Centranthus ruber* var. *coccineus*
23 *Lonicera henryi*
24 *Hedera colchica* 'Sulphur Heart'
25 *Solanum laxum* 'Album'

other ideas

WILDLIFE BORDER WITH YEAR-ROUND INTEREST

The main flowering period in a wildlife border is from late spring until early autumn, although evergreens, such as the skimmia, euphorbia, hebes, and the climbing honeysuckle and ivy, give some structure in the winter. Bulbs, particularly those that flower from late winter to early spring, are the simplest way to extend the season yet keep the basic plant associations. Of these, *Galanthus nivalis* (snowdrop) and the yellow-flowered *Eranthis hyemalis* (winter-flowering aconite) are the earliest. They are both low-growing, not reaching more than 10–15cm (4–6in) high, and very effective planted between the perennials at the front of the border. The hardy pinkish-purple *Cyclamen coum*, also best at the front of the border, can flower from late autumn right through to mid-spring. For height further back, the slightly taller species *Narcissus* are ideal – one of the earliest and most reliable is *N.* 'February Gold', which grows to about 25cm (10in) tall, and the earlier *N.* 'January Gold'. Place the tiny forms, like *N. bulbocodium* subsp. *bulbocodium* var. *conspicuus* and *N.* 'Canaliculatus', 10–15cm (4–6in), at the front. Crocuses are invaluable – traditional ones are the earliest, such as the violet *C. tommasinianus* 'Ruby Giant' (**pictured above**) and *C. chrysanthus* 'Snow Bunting' (white), with large-flowered hybrids slightly later in yellow, white, gold, blue and purple. *Colchicum* species (autumn crocus) provide large, dramatic flowers in autumn.

- option 3
Single-colour Border

Beds and borders planned to have a single colour can be incredibly dramatic when they are well done, but they are usually most effective when they are part of a much larger garden.

White is particularly successful, partly because it does not fight against the greens and other foliage colours. White gardens and borders are invariably more restful and relaxing than those consisting of brighter colours such as red or orange.

The success of this white border is due in part to the careful selection and placing of plants, most of which

have white flowers but which display tremendous diversity in size, shape and leaf. It is also due to the spread of flowering times to make the period of interest as long as possible.

Early in the year the soft leafy clumps and pure white flowers of *Pulmonaria* 'Sissinghurst White' are preceded by the ubiquitous *Helleborus niger* (Christmas rose). There is plenty of summer interest, including the long-flowering *Campanula persicifolia* var. *alba* and the tall, dramatic spikes of *Verbascum chaixii* 'Album'. The brilliant silver cut leaves of *Artemisia ludoviciana* 'Valerie Finnis' are a foil to the arching, variegated leaves and

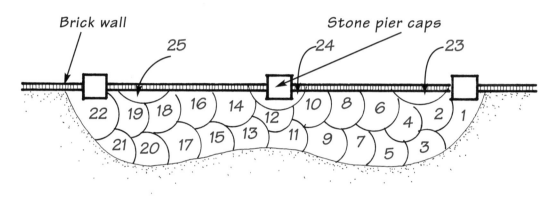

L A W N

planting key

1 *Spiraea betulifolia* var. *aemiliana*
2 *Campanula persicifolia* var. *alba*
3 *Aster novi-belgii* 'Snowsprite'
4 *Miscanthus sinensis* 'Morning Light'
5 *Pulmonaria* 'Sissinghurst White'
6 *Iris* 'White City'
7 *Holcus mollis* 'Albovariegatus'
8 *Crambe cordifolia*
9 *Lavandula angustifolia* 'Nana Alba'

10 *Delphinium* Galahad Group
11 *Pulmonaria* 'Sissinghurst White'
12 *Scabiosa caucasica* 'Miss Willmott'
13 *Kniphofia* 'Little Maid'
14 *Phlox paniculata* 'White Admiral'
15 *Helleborus niger*
16 *Digitalis purpurea* f. *albiflora*
17 *Tradescantia* × *andersoniana* 'Osprey'
18 *Verbascum chaixii* 'Album'

19 *Miscanthus sinensis* var. *condensatus* 'Cosmopolitan'
20 *Platycodon grandiflorus* f. *albus*
21 *Anemone sylvestris*
22 *Artemisia ludoviciana* 'Valerie Finnis'
23 *Clematis* 'Henryi'
24 *Jasminum stephanense*
25 *Rosa* 'Madame Alfred Carrière'

stiff, upright stems and striped leaves of *Miscanthus sinensis* var. *condensatus* 'Cosmopolitan'. Background fragrance is supplied for a long period by the climbing *Jasminum stephanense* on the wall, and nearer the front by the dwarf white lavender, *Lavandula angustifolia* 'Nana Alba'. Equally dramatic on the wall are *Clematis* 'Henryi', with its enormous chocolate-centred white stars, and the climbing rose *Rosa* 'Madame Alfred Carrière'.

On mid-season clematis, such as *Clematis* 'Henryi', prune a few stems lightly at about 2m (6ft) and the rest harder in early or mid-spring. This will give you some early flowers followed by a second flush later in the year.

Planning Beds and Borders

The size and shape of the beds and borders in your garden can have a significant impact on the overall effect and appearance of the garden, and it is therefore worth considering them carefully before you begin to mark them out and plant them up. Decide which style or border will reflect your garden's style.

Borders with straight edges and right-angled corners are rigid and geometric and impart a formal feeling to the garden. If you were to make the same border with a wavy edge, curving around the corners, you would achieve a much softer effect, even if you used the same species of plant.

The depth of borders – that is, the distance from front to back – is equally important. Narrow borders, of 90cm (36in) or less, whether they are formal or informal, will limit the number and size of plants you can successfully grow. Large plants, such as some viburnums and philadelphus, will appear out of proportion and awkward in a narrow border and will overhang your lawn or patio. For such a narrow border you should limit your choice to smaller plants or those with a slim habit of

growth. This has the effect of making your boundary fence, hedge or wall appear more prominent.

A deeper border, on the other hand, will allow you to grow larger plants at the back to hide the boundaries and smaller ones at the front to give a natural progression of heights.

plant group

PERENNIALS

A perennial may be defined as any plant that continues to grow from the same root system year by year but does not possess a woody structure. Some perennials, such as bergenia, euphorbia and *Vinca minor* (lesser periwinkle), are evergreen, but most are not, such as traditional varieties of lupins and delphiniums. These die down each autumn, leaving a below-ground crown or system of roots from which leaves, stems and flowers sprout again in the following season.

Perennials are favoured because they provide a huge range of colour, texture and size for the garden. It is possible to have perennials in flower somewhere in the garden almost all year round, beginning in late winter with the bright yellow of *Adonis amurensis* and pale lavender-blue of *Iris unguicularis*, and continue through until the late, bright red, autumn flowers of *Schizostylis coccinea* (Kaffir lily, **pictured above**).

While many perennials have bold, outstanding flowers – tall bearded iris, *Kniphofia* cultivars (red-hot poker) and peonies – others are equally attractive for their foliage colour or form, such as the beautiful dark purple of *Heuchera micrantha* var. *diversifolia* 'Palace Purple', the soft silver-greys of artemisia, and the silvers, greens and blues of hostas.

Perennials can be used for infilling and edging borders and beds, and as groundcover under and around trees and shrubs.

Island Beds

An island bed is simply an area of planting surrounded by lawn or hard landscaping, such as brick paving or gravel. They are an excellent way of displaying a selection of plants to the best effect because of the space and light around them, and access for maintenance is much easier.

There is no limit on how large or small the bed should be. What is more critical is that it should be in scale with the garden or space within which it is set – a 1.8m (6ft) diameter bed placed in the centre of 0.5 hectares (1.2 acres) of grass will be completely lost, while a bed that entirely fills a 15x20m (50x65ft) suburban garden apart from a surrounding 1m (about 3ft) strip of grass will be completely overpowering.

Apart from scale, the other main factor to consider is the relative heights of the plants compared to the size of the bed. As a rule, the height of the tallest plants should not be more than about half the width of the bed itself, so an oval bed 6m (20ft) long by 3m (10ft) wide should not contain any plants that will grow higher than 1.5m (5ft) in order to maintain a harmonious balance. This balance is also maintained by making sure that you grade your island-bed plants by keeping the lowest ones at the edge and gradually increasing in height towards the centre, where the tallest ones will be planted.

• option 1

Flower Arranger's Island Bed

For easy maintenance, particularly when it is set in the middle of a lawn, the shape of your island bed should be kept simple, avoiding corners and tight curves wherever possible.

This example is of an oval bed approximately 3.3m (11ft) long by 2.4m (8ft) wide. It has been thoughtfully planned so that it makes a striking feature from early spring until late autumn, and at the same time provides material suitable for cutting and flower arranging.

A holly, *Ilex aquifolium* 'Ferox Argentea', together with *Spiraea japonica* 'Gold Mound' and *Berberis thunbergii* 'Dart's Red Lady' provide a shrubby background to a collection of reliable, long-lived perennials. The sunny side of the bed includes plants suited to the warmer,

drier conditions that will be found here, such as *Achillea* 'Moonshine' and *Agapanthus* 'Blue Baby'. On the other side, however, the soil will be slightly shaded by the taller plants in the centre, including the holly, and the cooler, moister conditions here are better suited to plants such as *Hosta* 'Frances Williams' and *Astilbe* 'Sprite'.

On drier soils, the hosta, astilbe and hellebore are likely to be less successful, so you should include some suitable, drought-resistant alternatives here – some possibilities to consider include the golden-variegated comfrey, *Symphytum* 'Goldsmith', the spreading (but easily controlled) *Persicaria affinis* 'Superba' with its pink pokers and, as long as there is reasonable direct sunlight, the silver-blue, cut leaves and thistle flowers of *Eryngium variifolium* (sea holly).

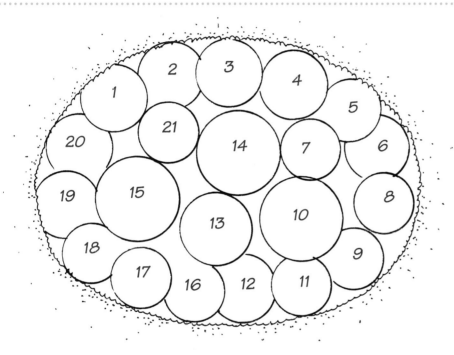

other ideas

FLOWER ARRANGER'S GARDEN IN SHADE

The flower arranger's island bed is suitable for an open position in sun on well-drained soils. In a slightly shadier position, you might need to change some of the plants that would otherwise not perform to their full potential. Fleshy and grey-leaved plants, such as the sedum and achillea, would need to be replaced, perhaps with *Anemone hupehensis* var. *japonica* 'Bressingham Glow' and *Acanthus mollis*. Similarly, the dianthus (pink) and nepeta (catmint) could be replaced by edging plants, such as *Lamium maculatum* 'Pink Pewter' (deadnettle) and *Geranium himalayense* 'Gravetye'. *Campanula lactiflora* 'Pouffe' would be a better alternative to the agapanthus, and *Berberis thunbergii* 'Aurea' prefers a lightly shaded position and is therefore more suitable than the spiraea.

The winter-flowering *Iris unguicularis* needs full sun to flower well, so instead try *Iris foetidissima* 'Variegata', whose winter interest is its variegated leaves and orange seed pods.

If foliage is required for flower arrangements you can quite easily introduce a number of plants to satisfy this need – *Artemisia* 'Powis Castle' for its soft grey foliage in place of the sedum, the cream, red and green *Houttuynia cordata* 'Chameleon' (**pictured above**) instead of the *Euphorbia polychroma* and, perhaps, another hosta, such as the golden-leaved *H.* 'August Moon' instead of the astilbe.

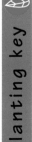

planting key

1 *Sedum spectabile* 'Iceberg'
2 *Helleborus niger*
3 *Astilbe* 'Sprite'
4 *Hosta* 'Frances Williams'
5 *Euphorbia polychroma*
6 *Dicentra* 'Luxuriant'
7 *Iris sibirica* 'White Swirl'
8 *Aster novi-belgii* 'Lady in Blue'
9 *Iris unguicularis*
10 *Berberis thunbergii* 'Dart's Red Lady'
11 *Bergenia* 'Sunningdale'
12 *Achillea* 'Moonshine'
13 *Phlox paniculata* 'Prince of Orange'
14 *Ilex aquifolium* 'Ferox Argentea'
15 *Spiraea japonica* 'Gold Mound'
16 *Doronicum* 'Miss Mason'
17 *Agapanthus* 'Blue Baby'
18 *Leucanthemum* × *superbum* 'Snowcap'
19 *Dianthus* 'Doris'
20 *Nepeta* × *faassenii*
21 *Crocosmia* 'Lucifer'

● **option 2**

Foliage Island Bed

It is not only flowers that make a plant attractive —
there are many species and cultivars whose appeal
lies in the size, shape, colour and texture of their
leaves and whose flowers are of lesser importance.
This design for an island bed deliberately uses such
foliage plants to create a composition that illustrates
the above features admirably.

The variegated *Berberis thunbergii* 'Harlequin',
Viburnum davidii and *Phormium* 'Yellow Wave' provide
a permanent woody and evergreen framework and
backdrop to a selection of perennials that are chosen
primarily for their foliage. In addition to variations in
colour, such as the purple leaves and yellow flowers of
Lysimachia ciliata 'Firecracker' and the soft, hairy, silver-
grey foliage of *Stachys byzantina* 'Silver Carpet' (lamb's

ears), there are contrasts in leaf shape in the thistle-like leaves of *Eryngium variifolium* (sea holly) and the sword-shaped, silver-striped, spikes of *Iris foetidissima* 'Variegata'. The warm, drier side of the bed is ideal for the sun-loving *Ballota pseudodictamnus*, while the blue-leaved *Hosta* 'Halcyon' and apple-green *Alchemilla mollis* (lady's mantle) thrive on the cooler shady side, where they are partly sheltered by the taller plants at the centre of the bed. Although they are secondary to the foliage in this example, there is still some flower interest: the delicately veined, pale lavender saucers of *Geranium renardii*, the pure white 'dead-nettle' flowers of tiny ground-hugging *Lamium maculatum* 'White Nancy', the greeny yellow clusters of *Alchemilla mollis* and the bold red spikes of *Bergenia* Wintermärchen set against its glossy, dark red-tinged leaves in late winter.

planting key

1 *Iris foetidissima* 'Variegata'
2 *Bergenia* 'Wintermärchen'
3 *Hosta* 'Halcyon'
4 *Alchemilla mollis*
5 *Dryopteris erythrosora*
6 *Melissa officinalis* 'Aurea'
7 *Lysimachia ciliata* 'Firecracker'
8 *Festuca glauca* 'Blauglut'
9 *Ajuga reptans* 'Variegata'
10 *Berberis thunbergii* 'Harlequin'
11 *Heuchera micrantha* var. *diversifolia* 'Palace Purple'
12 *Ballota pseudodictamnus*
13 *Eryngium variifolium*
14 *Phormium* 'Yellow Wave'
15 *Viburnum davidii*
16 *Ophiopogon planiscapus* 'Nigrescens'
17 *Stachys byzantina* 'Silver Carpet'
18 *Carex oshimensis* 'Evergold'
19 *Geranium renardii*
20 *Lamium maculatum* 'White Nancy'
21 *Helleborus argutifolius*

other ideas

FOLIAGE EFFECTS

In the most successful gardens, foliage is given as much thought as flowers and can sometimes be used as a backdrop to set off other plants. The purple leaves of *Cotinus coggygria* Rubrifolius group behind the silver filigree foliage and sulphur-yellow flowers of *Achillea* 'Moonshine' or the large, bold foliage of the climber *Vitis coignetiae* perfectly set off the slender upright flower spikes of *Cimicifuga simplex* var. *matsumurae* 'White Pearl'. Bright splashes of foliage, particularly gold or yellow, can be used to lift an otherwise drab corner – the dogwood *Cornus alba* 'Aurea', if the soil is not too dry, for example, or the evergreen *Taxus baccata* 'Semperaurea', where it is drier.

The form and shape of foliage plants are equally important. Compare the stiff, architectural texture of the large mahonias, *M. x media* 'Winter Sun' and *M. lomariifolia*, with the grassy, slender-stemmed colours of small-leaved bamboos, such as *Fargesia murieliae* 'Simba' and *F. nitida* (**pictured above**), swaying in the breeze. Strong, horizontal forms are equally important for contrast and balance, such as *Juniperus pfitzeriana* 'Old Gold', or the taller dogwood *Cornus controversa* 'Variegata', with its striking tiers of silver-edged foliage.

Plants that provide interest in flower and foliage are particularly valuable, such as *Weigela* 'Victoria' with dark purple-green leaves and deep rose-pink flowers.

• **option 3**

Single-colour Island Bed

This island bed is designed with an emphasis on pinks and purples.

As with all island beds, taller plants are placed towards the centre. In this case, the three main plants – *Berberis thunbergii* 'Kobold', the evergreen azalea *Rhododendron* 'Palestrina' and *Ballota* 'All Hallows Green' – have been deliberately chosen for their pale green foliage, which acts as a foil and contrast to the richer, darker colours around them. Around the edge of the bed occasional splashes of silver and grey are used to the same effect. These include *Artemisia alba* 'Canescens' and the furry-leaved *Stachys byzantina* 'Silver Carpet' (lamb's ears).

There is a good balance between both foliage and flower interest, which adds an extra dimension to the design. Some flowers are small and delicate, such as the purple-blue of *Viola riviniana* Purpurea Group, while others, such as the giant purple globes of *Allium giganteum*, are bold. Further interest is created by variations in the habit and form of the plants – the stiff

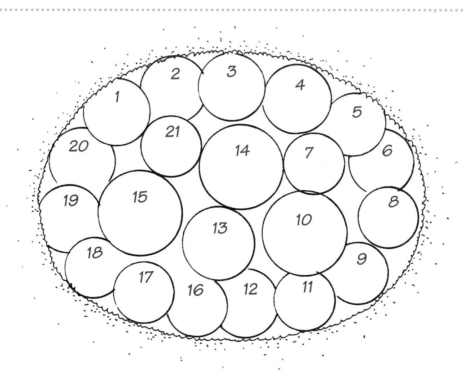

planting key

1 *Trifolium repens* 'Purpurascens'
2 *Dicentra* 'Bountiful'
3 *Ajuga reptans* 'Atropurpurea'
4 *Iris* 'Green Spot'
5 *Allium roseum*
6 *Stachys byzantina* 'Silver Carpet'
7 *Aquilegia vulgaris* var. *stellata* 'Ruby Port'
8 *Heuchera* 'Rachel'

9 *Tradescantia andersoniana* 'Pauline'
10 *Berberis thunbergii* 'Kobold'
11 *Platycodon grandiflorus* 'Perlmutterschale'
12 *Iris* 'Blue Pigmy'
13 *Artemisia alba* 'Canescens'
14 *Rhododendron* 'Palestrina' (evergreen azalea)
15 *Ballota* 'All Hallows Green'

16 *Sedum telephium* 'Matrona'
17 *Viola riviniana* Purpurea Group
18 *Festuca glauca* 'Blaufuchs'
19 *Aster amellus* 'Veilchenkönigin'
20 *Ophiopogon planiscapus* 'Nigrescens'
21 *Allium giganteum*

upright leaves of the intermediate bearded *Iris* 'Green Spot' and the standard dwarf bearded *Iris* 'Blue Pigmy', the thick fleshy purple-tinged stems of the late-flowering *Sedum telephium* 'Matrona' and the hedgehog-

like mounds of fine, steel-blue leaves of *Festuca glauca* 'Blaufuchs'.

Although this is really a seasonal bed, the period of interest is prolonged. It begins in spring with the purple-blue spikes and dark foliage of *Ajuga reptans* 'Atropurpurea' and continues right through to autumn with the yellow-centred daisies of *Aster amellus* 'Veilchenkönigin' and the large, pink heads of *Sedum telephium* 'Matrona'.

The bold heads of alliums such as a *Giganteum* are striking when in full flower, but are equally dramatic when dead, lasting right though late autumn, and can be used for fresh or dried flower arrangements.

plant group

ORNAMENTAL GRASSES

Some ornamental grasses form neat, striking clumps that are ideal for planting in island beds, as they look equally good from all angles, and they can set off other, flowering plants to excellent effect. They vary widely in size and colour, and many are evergreen, providing year-round interest. There are grasses that produce beautiful flowerheads or seedheads, and others that rustle soothingly in the breeze. Winter frost or spring dew can highlight their statuesque shapes, introducing a whole new design element to the garden.

Festuca glauca (blue fescue, **pictured above**) is an evergreen perennial grass with dense clumps, up to 30cm (1ft) tall, of narrow, upright leaves that have a distinct blue tinge to them. *F. glauca* 'Blaufuchs' and 'Elijah Blue' both have eye-catching blue foliage, and are ideal for small gardens. They produce flower spikes in early summer. *Stipa* species make fine, larger specimen plants, with their attractive, feathery flowerheads produced during the summer months.

The distinctive *Uncinia Rubra* (New Zealand Hook Sedge) is another clump-forming perennial, evergreen grass suitable for small gardens, growing to 30cm tall and wide. Its leaves are mahogany red, sometimes taking on orange tints. This plant can be grown in various settings: as a specimen in its own right; as part of a colour-themed design; in containers; and as a foil for other grasses or flowering plants.

Creating a Focal Point

Some gardens, especially those that are long and narrow, can present a challenge because they tend to be dominated by the side boundaries, and the view is channelled straight to the far end, providing little interest or stimulus. An island bed, used as a feature that effectively divides the garden into two distinct areas, linked by gravel paths, can provide the answer to this problem by drawing the eye away from the end and sides of the plot.

The island bed could be planted up in any of the ways described in options 1, 2 and 3, or you could plant groups of individual shrubs, making sure that some of them are evergreen so that you retain the effect even in winter. The planting design of the island bed should be reflected in and complemented by the choice of plants for the boundary beds and borders, so that the garden becomes a coherent whole, with a natural focal point in the centre that is equally attractive viewed from any side.

You should also try to soften and disguise the long boundaries so that the rigid shape is less easy to discern. Simply using climbers on the

wall or fence will just convert it into what is effectively a 'hedge'. Use some shrubs with plenty of width to relieve the vertical flatness and taller, upright plants to break up the horizontal line along the top of the boundary.

Corner Beds

Corner beds are an efficient way of achieving some relatively large-scale planting in an otherwise modest space without the design being out of scale or claustrophobic. A narrow, perimeter border of the same area along, say, two or three sides of the same garden would not be as effective because the tall, large shrubs at the back would be overpowering. When enclosed on two sides by solid barriers, say the walls of a building, corner beds can also be a great way to create plantings suited to particular microclimates – for example, a cool, shady corner filled with bold-leaved hostas, feathery astilbes and delicate ferns or a hot, sunny spot containing exotic *Passiflora* species (passionflower), *Jasminum* species (jasmine) and agapanthus.

For the best dramatic effect, the planting should be tiered, with the lowest plants at the front and becoming progressively taller towards the back. The quarter-circular corner bed shown overleaf also has a small tree, not quite in the far corner, for added height and as a focal point. Rather than solid walls, the bed is enclosed by a fence made of arched trellis panels to let as much light through as possible for the benefit of the plants and also to provide ready-made support for climbers at the back. At the front of the bed is a mowing strip made from thin pieces of natural stone at least 15cm (6in) wide. This not only allows you to cut the grass easily without going over on to the bed itself, but also provides a platform for low edging plants to spill on to and be seen to best effect.

• option 1

Mediterranean Corner Bed

In many gardens you will find that there are hot, dry corners at the junction of fences, walls or hedges. These areas have a tendency to act as sun traps and so they are ideal for creating Mediterranean-style plantings, particularly where they are sheltered from cold winds and is fairly free-draining.

Plants with silver-grey or leathery leaves are quite tolerant of heat and a degree of dryness, and these qualities typify many Mediterranean plants. The large *Cistus* × *hybridus* (rock rose) is a perfect example: it has wind- and sun-resistant foliage and small white flowers resembling single roses. Alongside this is the equally tolerant, narrow grey-green foliage of *Rosmarinus officinalis* 'Miss Jessopp's Upright', with its pale blue

flowers in spring. *Spartium junceum* (Spanish broom) requires a lot of space, but it rewards the correct conditions with a continuous display of large, yellow, pea-like flowers on rush-like stems. Providing a dramatic, early focal point is a *Cercis siliquastrum* (Judas tree), which bears clusters of small, pink pea-like flowers on naked stems in early spring.

Many herbs originate from the countries of the Mediterranean, and the ornamental forms of these make good additions to the garden – the soft, feathery haze *Foeniculum vulgare* 'Giant Bronze' (bronze fennel), the purple, felty leaves of *Salvia officinalis* 'Purpurascens' (purple sage) and, right at the front, the low, creeping *Thymus serpyllum* 'Pink Chintz' (thyme). Bulbs are also native to these regions, some small and delicate, while others, like the large, purplish heads of *Allium schubertii*, are dramatic.

plant group

HERBS

Herbs (see also pp.60–61) range from annuals and biennials to perennials and shrubs; what unites them as a group is the fact that they are suitable for use in cooking and medicine, and even for producing perfumes and cosmetics. The leaves are often fragrant, especially when rubbed or crushed. A wide range of attractive species and cultivars is now available.

Many herbs hail originally from dry, scrubby Mediterranean regions, and these are ideal for growing in hot, dry situations. In general, herbs with silver, hairy or needle-shaped leaves, such as lavender, rosemary and sage (**pictured above**) are sun-lovers, but some herbs prefer a degree of shade. These tend to be the ones with wider, green leaves, such as mint. Make sure when grouping plants together that they have similar requirements for soil, light and so on; otherwise one plant may swamp another.

You can treat the cultivation of herbs in a variety of ways: dedicate a special area to them, mix them in with other ornamental plants in beds and borders, or grow them in a raised bed or a series of containers. For the sake of convenience, it is a good idea to site any plants suitable for culinary use near to the kitchen. When harvesting herbs, do not take too much from the plant at any one time, as this can halt its growth. It is better to grow a number of specimens of the same herb together, so that no one plant is over-harvested.

Small tree · Trellis screen · Stone edging strip · LAWN

planting key

1 *Cercis siliquastrum*
2 *Spartium junceum*
3 *Foeniculum vulgare* 'Giant Bronze'
4 *Rosmarinus officinalis* 'Miss Jessopp's Upright'
5 *Cistus × hybridus*
6 *Allium schubertii*
7 *Lavandula intermedia* 'Grappenhall'
8 *Genista hispanica*
9 *Acanthus spinosus*
10 *Salvia officinalis* 'Purpurascens'
11 *Helianthemum* 'The Bride'
12 *Thymus serpyllum* 'Pink Chintz'
13 *Daphne cneorum*
14 *Stachys byzantina* 'Primrose Heron'
15 *Trachelospermum jasminoides* 'Variegatum'
16 *Vitis vinifera* 'Incana'

BEDS AND BORDERS

37

• option 2

Moist, Shady Corner Bed

A shady corner bed with good, moisture-retentive soil offers an opportunity to grow a selection of plants that are not only individually garden-worthy but that, when put together, also make an extremely attractive composition.

Different characteristics of both flower and foliage are displayed here, from the huge, dinner-plate leaves of

Astilboides tabularis through the dark, almost polished, green leaves and perfect pink flowers of *Camellia* x *williamsii* 'Donation' to the tiny, leathery leaves of *Vaccinium vitis-idaea* (cowberry), with its pink-tinged, bell-shaped flowers and red autumn berries. Like many golden-leaved plants, *Filipendula ulmaria* 'Aurea' (meadowsweet) prefers a position out of sun, where it will make a lovely bright splash. Equally at home is the

dark purplish-red foliage of *Lobelia cardinalis* (cardinal flower) and its brilliant red flowers, although this is more often seen in the margins of ponds. The unusual evergreen climber *Berberidopsis corallina* (coral plant) prefers a cool, shady position in which to produce its almost artificial-looking, pendent, red flowers, as does the vigorous honeysuckle *Lonicera tellmanniana*, with its outstanding

clusters of coppery-yellow tubular flowers borne in midsummer.

Acer palmatum (Japanese maple) will grow reasonably well in most situations, but it is prone to scorching in full sun, especially if the soil becomes dry. Here, however, it makes a superb focal point, sheltered from the heat of the sun and the desiccating effect of cold winds by the combination of the enclosing trellis screen and the climbers growing on it.

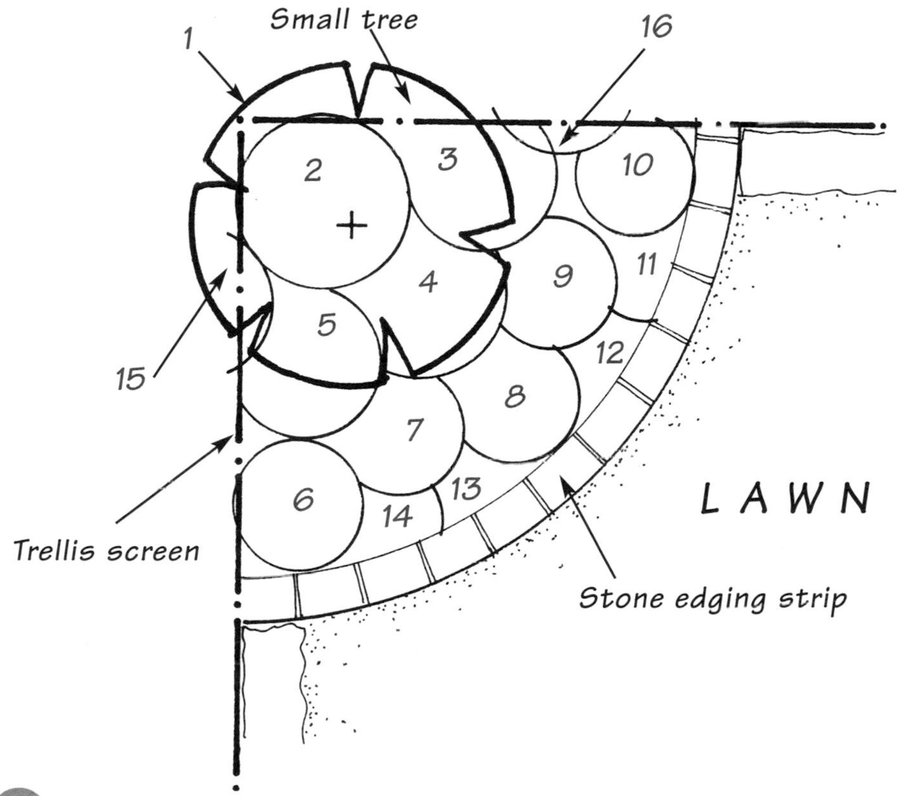

other ideas

SUNNY CORNER

To transform this moist shady corner bed to one positioned in full sun you will need to select plants that give an equally striking display, but are more tolerant of a hotter position.

The Japanese maple could be replaced by a snake-bark maple, such as *Acer grosseri* var. *hersii* or *A. rufinerve*. If it did not get morning sun after a hard frost, the camellia could stay, or replace it with a pink-flowered rhododendron, such as R. 'Alice'. Try *Hydrangea serrata* 'Bluebird' since 'Grayswood' prefers light shade. The golden-leaved form of meadow-sweet can scorch in full sun, so for a bright splash use the dainty, golden-leaved grass *Hakonechloa macra* 'Alboaurea' (**pictured above**). Although the hosta will grow in a sunny, moist position, its silver-blue leaves will not develop their full colour; you would be better with a similar coloured plant, such as H. 'Frances Williams', which has a buff edge to the leaves. The evergreen climber *Berberidopsis corallina* (coral plant) needs some shade, or at least to be out of direct sun to thrive and flower properly, so for a position in full sun use a vigorous clematis, such as C. *flammula*, with its myriad tiny, late, white flowers. Similarly, *Lonicera tellmanniana* thrives in light or even full shade, but some honeysuckles are happy in sun provided that their roots are cool and moist, so use the purplish-red L. *periclymenum* 'Serotina' or the creamy-yellow 'Graham Thomas'.

Diagram labels:

Small tree
1
16
2
3
10
15
4
5
9
11
12
8
7
6
14
13
LAWN
Trellis screen
Stone edging strip

---

planting key

1 *Acer palmatum*
2 *Camellia* × *williamsii* 'Donation'
3 *Cornus alba* 'Elegantissima'
4 *Hydrangea serrata* 'Grayswood'
5 *Enkianthus campanulatus*
6 *Skimmia laureola*
7 *Kirengeshoma palmata*
8 *Astilboides tabularis*

9 *Lobelia* 'Queen Victoria'
10 *Filipendula ulmaria* 'Aurea'
11 *Vaccinium vitis-idaea*
12 *Carex morrowii* 'Fisher's Form'
13 *Primula japonica* 'Postford White'
14 *Hosta* 'Halcyon'
15 *Berberidopsis corallina*
16 *Lonicera tellmanniana*

- option 3

Corner Bed for Wildlife

There is an argument that a large, concentrated mass of appropriate plants provides a better habitat for wildlife than a number of individual ones dotted about on their own.

Certainly, in terms of the amount of cover and shelter created, this would seem likely, and the evergreen *Osmanthus burkwoodii* at the back of this bed suits the

purpose admirably. It also flowers early in spring, and its fragrant blooms provide some of the first insect food of the year. Almost as early, *Clematis montana* var. *rubens* 'Elizabeth' makes a mass of stem and leaves all over the trellis screen, which is ideal for nesting and roosting birds, and the hundreds of simple pink flowers are also rich in pollen.

Plenty of spring food will boost the insect population,

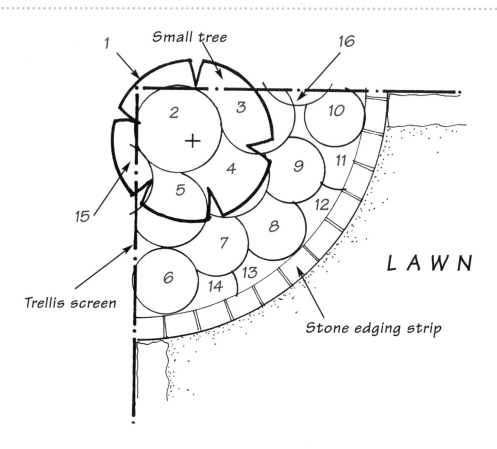

1 *Sorbus hupehensis*
2 *Osmanthus burkwoodii*
3 *Cotoneaster simonsii*
4 *Rosa* 'Bonica'
5 *Rhododendron* 'Gibraltar' (deciduous azalea)
6 *Galtonia candicans*

7 *Sedum telephium* 'Matrona'
8 *Chrysanthemum* 'Clara Curtis'
9 *Erica erigena* 'Brightness'
10 *Origanum vulgare* 'Aureum'
11 *Salvia* × *sylvestris* 'Mainacht'
12 *Viola* 'Princesse de Galles'

13 *Pachysandra terminalis* 'Variegata'
14 *Hebe* 'Wingletye'
15 *Clematis montana* var. *rubens* 'Elizabeth'
16 *Lonicera implexa*

which is good for insectivorous birds such as warblers, so spring-flowering plants are an important part of the bed. The deciduous azalea *Rhododendron* 'Gibraltar', which has scented, orange-pink trumpets, the large, upright heather *Erica erigena* 'Brightness' and the diminutive, but nonetheless valuable,

purple-flowered *Viola odorata* will attract insects and provide the essential early-season boost. A steady trickle of sustenance appears over the course of the summer – the bees' favourite, *Salvia* x *sylvestris* 'Mainacht', the lovely, long-flowering pink shrub rose *Rosa* 'Bonica' and the unusual summer-flowering bulb *Galtonia candicans*.

Later, food is needed to enable wildlife to survive winter. Here there are berries for birds – the waxy white clusters on *Sorbus hupehensis* (Hubei rowan), the blackbird's favourite *Cotoneaster simonsii*, with its red fruits, and the dark, purplish-red sticky berries of *Lonicera implexa*, which is doubly valued for the earlier fragrant, nectar-rich flowers.

Rosa 'Bonica' is one of the most reliable and troublefree shrub roses with masses of neat, pink flowers for many weeks.

Planting for Wildlife

Even the smallest garden can be made more acceptable to a wide range of wildlife, but for best results it will need to provide not only adequate food resources but also a suitable habitat for shelter, nesting and hibernation.

Mixed borders will provide some cover all year round, and the more generous they are the more wildlife they are likely to attract. For a steady supply of food, make your garden a year-round one, beginning in winter with the flowers of mahonia, viburnum and heather. In spring there should be masses of bulbs, one or two flowering trees and early perennials, especially alpines. Make sure there are abundant summer flowers and, in autumn, fruit, berries and seeds.

Provide overwintering and roosting habitats for small birds – for instance, a large variegated ivy, such as *Hedera colchica* 'Dentata Variegata' mixed with *Houttuynia cordata*. A pile of old logs, bricks or stones is better for amphibians,

although it must be out of sight – beneath or behind an evergreen shrub, such as *Viburnum tinus* (laurustinus), at the back of a bed is ideal.

You must include water – at least a birdbath for drinking, and preferably a small, shallow-sided pond in which amphibians and water-loving insects can complete their lifecycles.

BERRYING PLANTS

Plants that have ornamental berries and fruits are an excellent way to extend interest in the garden into the autumn and beyond, and they also provide valuable food for local wildlife.

Some perennials produce attractive fruits – the brilliant orange seed pods of *Iris foetidissima* (stinking gladwyn) are ideal for brightening up a dark shady corner – but the greatest range is usually found in shrubs and trees. Colours can vary from white through a range of yellows and oranges to red, purples, black and even blue, as found in the startling bean-like pods of *Decaisnea fargesii* and the tiny, perfect spheres of the pretty climber *Ampelopsis glandulosa* var. *brevipedunculata* 'Elegans'. The rose family contains many excellent berrying plants, not only such roses as the large bush *Rosa* 'Geranium' but also shrubs such as *Pyracantha* and *Cotoneaster* species, such as *C. frigidus* 'Cornubia' (**pictured above**), which have orange, yellow and red berries; crab apples, such as *Malus zumi* 'Golden Hornet' and *M. robusta* 'Red Sentinel', with, respectively, small yellow and red apples, which often hang on the tree well after leaf fall, and *Sorbus*, a genus including the mountain ashes and whitebeams. Perhaps the most startling and long-lasting berries, however, are found on the evergreen shrub *Gaultheria mucronata*. Female plants produce amazing white, pink or red marble-sized berries that last right through the winter. Remember to plant a male variety, such as 'Thymfolia' to pollinate.

Raised Beds

A raised bed is, in reality, nothing more than a large container, and it has the same requirements – that is, ample good drainage, an appropriate growing medium or compost and the means of containing such a medium within a rigid, durable structure, which could be brick, stone, concrete or wood. Raised beds are an excellent way of providing relief in a flat area, especially where tall or large plants would be out of keeping – on the sunny edge of a patio or terrace, for example. As with more traditional containers, they can be used in situations where it is impossible to plant directly into the ground or where the existing soil is not suitable for the type of plants you may wish to grow. Raised beds are, for example, an ideal way of growing alpines, which require relatively friable, free-draining soil, where the natural ground is heavy, sticky clay.

The raised bed in the design shown overleaf is made from recycled wooden railway sleepers, which are laid on top of each other with the ends staggered. To make the feature more interesting, it is in a broad L-shaped arrangement that overlaps the corner of a patio. The brick edge of the patio is continued to create a small square of gravel and stones, which is partly enclosed by the raised bed and on which two or three brightly planted containers are placed as a contrast to the strong, horizontal lines of the dark timbers. Plants with a naturally prostrate or trailing habit, which will spill over the top of the bed, are mixed with other more upright forms to give balance and variety. Planting around the back of the raised bed is deliberately kept at a low level to allow the full effect of the plants within it to be appreciated from all sides.

• option 1

Raised Bed with Year-round Interest

A successful year-round bed or border relies on a complementary mixture of flowers and foliage in order to be most effective.

In this particular raised bed, which achieves this aim, the plants have also been selected according to their growth rates and habit, so that they make an attractive overall composition in which the characteristics of individual plants are not swamped by their neighbours.

In even the smallest gardens an evergreen framework is essential, and here it is provided by dwarf conifers – the neat, blue-green globe of *Thuja occidentalis* 'Danica', the beautiful feathery gold pillar of *Juniperus communis* 'Schneverdingen Goldmachangel' and the pyramidal mound of pale sulphur and green of *Chamaecyparis lawsoniana* 'Pygmaea Argentea'.

Raised beds are excellent ways of displaying creeping and trailing plants. *Helianthemum* 'Wisley Primrose', *Cotoneaster congestus* 'Nanus' and *Juniperus pfitzeriana* 'Gold Sovereign' spill over and soften the timber edge. Winter-flowering heathers fit perfectly into this scheme: the deep red flowers and bronze-green foliage of *Erica carnea* 'Myretoun Ruby' and the more prostrate gold foliage and pale pink flowers of *E. carnea* 'Foxhollow' provide colour for weeks in late winter.

Alpines appreciate the good drainage in a raised bed and are in scale with the dwarf conifers and shrubs. The beautiful dark-veined pink flowers of *Geranium cinereum* 'Ballerina', the long-flowering *Rhodanthemum hosmariense*, with its cheerful daisies, and the spreading, white-flowered evergreen *Arabis ferdinandi-coburgi* 'Old Gold' will all thrive here.

plant group

ALPINES

In its broadest sense an alpine is really a dwarf perennial. Some alpines are deciduous – *Pulsatilla vulgaris* (pasqueflower), for example – and die right down each winter, but many, particularly fleshy-leaved plants, including sedums and sempervivums, are evergreen.

Many alpines originate from upland, mountainous areas, where they grow in shallow, gritty, free-draining soil or even directly in the small stones or scree found at the base of steep slopes. The ideal conditions for alpines in a garden should, therefore, try to mimic those found in nature, and their size and growing needs make them perfect for growing in sunny rockeries and scree gardens where space is limited. Where ground conditions are cold and wet, they can be successfully grown in almost any type of container, from the smallest terracotta pot through to large raised beds.

Some alpines, such as the pink-flowered *Geranium cinereum* and the dwarf willowherb, *Epilobium glabellum*, flower throughout summer and occasionally into autumn. The majority, however, are at their peak of interest from late winter through to the end of spring, and, if interplanted with early-flowering dwarf bulbs, such as *Galanthus* species (snowdrop), crocus and *Iris reticulata* or *I. danfordiae*, they can make an eye-catching display before the larger shrubs and perennials really come into their own.

Timber raised bed (e.g. railway sleepers)

Brick edging

Pots

PATIO

Stones/pebbles

planting key

1 *Geranium cinereum* 'Ballerina'
2 *Rhodanthemum hosmariense*
3 *Dianthus* 'Garland'
4 *Hebe* 'Youngii'
5 *Helianthemum* 'Wisley Primrose'
6 *Thuja occidentalis* 'Danica'
7 *Erica carnea* 'Myretoun Ruby'
8 *Juniperus communis* 'Schneverdingen Goldmachangel'
9 *Persicaria vacciniifolia*
10 *Berberis thunbergii* 'Bagatelle'
11 *Campanula carpatica* var. *turbinata* 'Karl Foerster'
12 *Cotoneaster congestus* 'Nanus'
13 *Arabis ferdinandi-coburgi* 'Old Gold'
14 *Tsuga canadensis* 'Jeddeloh'
15 *Festuca glauca* 'Elijah Blue'
16 *Chamaecyparis lawsoniana* 'Pygmaea Argentea'
17 *Erica carnea* 'Foxhollow'
18 *Lavandula angustifolia* 'Hidcote Pink'
19 *Juniperus pfitzeriana* 'Gold Sovereign'

● option 2

Low-maintenance Raised Bed

One of the attractions of a raised bed is that it provides easier access to the plants in it for routine maintenance. As a low-maintenance feature, it has a head start on more conventional borders.

The plants in this raised bed have been chosen so that, once established, maintenance is reduced to an absolute minimum. This is achieved by a combination of plants that are evergreen or that completely cover the soil as they grow. Some have both characteristics. The evergreen shrubs *Hebe ochracea* 'James Stirling', with its ochre-coloured, whipcord foliage, the dwarf, yellow-flowered *Rhododendron* 'Chikor' and the dense but neat, long-flowering *Parahebe lyallii* provide spots of height.

Ground-covering alpines are an important part of the planting. The early green-grey carpets of pink-flowering

Aubrieta 'Bressingham Pink' combine with the miniature *Alchemilla alpina* (alpine lady's mantle), with its gentle crown of soft, pale green leaves, and the long-flowering, weed-suppressing mound of *Viola* 'Jackanapes'.

Foliage also plays an important part in the scheme. There are the grassy, near-black evergreen leaves of *Ophiopogon planiscapus* 'Nigrescens' (black lilyturf); the long, spotted leaves of *Pulmonaria*

longifolia, with its dark blue spring flowers as a bonus, and the bright silver, white and green leaves of the miniature ivy *Hedera helix* 'Little Diamond'. Other plant associations are the silver-purple leaves of *Heuchera* 'Pewter Moon' beside the attractive flowers of *Corydalis flexuosa* 'China Blue'. Next to that are the almost unending tiny white flowers of *Epilobium glabellum* (dwarf willowherb) above a low mat of bright, glossy leaves.

plant group

GROUNDCOVER PLANTS

Groundcover in its literal sense is any plant that covers bare soil with leaves and stems. Often thought to be only low-growing or prostrate evergreens, such as *Hedera* species (ivy), *Vinca* species (periwinkle) and pachysandra, in fact the number of plants available to gardeners that can achieve the same effect is enormous.

First, they do not have to be evergreen. Leafy, deciduous perennials, such as hostas (**pictured above**), ligularia and *Symphytum* species (comfrey), make superb groundcovering mounds, as do astilbes and *Pulmonaria* species (lungwort). In addition, they need not be low-growing. Some of the best are large shrubs: *Viburnum tinus* (laurustinus), rhododendron hybrids and *Elaeagnus pungens* cultivars all make large specimens beneath which you will rarely find a weed!

Where space is limited, many alpines form low mats that, grown closely together, form delightful, weed-free displays. Probably the ultimate in groundcover, however, are the low-growing ornamental conifers, especially junipers, of which there are many forms, from the wide-spreading *Juniperus* × *pfitzeriana* 'Pfitzeriana Aurea' – one plant can cover 10 square metres (yards) – to the neat, bonsai-like elegance of *Tsuga canadensis* 'Jeddeloh', ideal for heather and conifer gardens and alpine beds. Heathers, too, make brilliant low groundcover, creating blocks of coloured foliage and flowers from late spring through to early winter.

Timber raised bed (e.g. railway sleepers)

Brick edging

Pots

Stones/pebbles

PATIO

planting key

1 *Ajuga reptans* 'Burgundy Glow'
2 *Erica vagans* 'Lyonesse'
3 *Aubrieta* 'Bressingham Pink'
4 *Hedera helix* 'Little Diamond'
5 *Bergenia* 'Bressingham Ruby'
6 *Rhododendron* 'Chikor'
7 *Epimedium* × *perralchicum* 'Frohnleiten'
8 *Hebe ochracea* 'James Stirling'
9 *Alchemilla alpina*
10 *Heuchera* 'Pewter Moon'
11 *Viola* 'Jackanapes'
12 *Pulmonaria longifolia*
13 *Artemisia schmidtiana* 'Nana'
14 *Ophiopogon planiscapus* 'Nigrescens'
15 *Arenaria montana*
16 *Parahebe lyallii*
17 *Corydalis flexuosa* 'China Blue'
18 *Epilobium glabellum*
19 *Thymus pulegioides* 'Bertram Anderson'

● option 3

Colour-themed Raised Bed

By their nature, raised beds tend to be located next to paths or other paved areas, where the delicate beauty of the plants in them can be seen and appreciated at close quarters and where there is easy access for the less-able gardener. Such positions do not, therefore, necessarily need to be filled with brightly coloured plants that demand attention. An excellent scheme for such a bed would be in pastel colours, to make a harmonious, relaxing display.

Here, such an effect is achieved using plants that individually are quite striking and are all the more interesting when examined close up. White is an essential colour in any kind of plant combination. Here it is found in the rock rose *Helianthemum* 'Wisley White', and the dwarf evergreen azalea *Rhododendron* 'Palestrina'. Neutral colours, such as silver or grey, are equally valuable in providing background and foils to other colours. The neat, soft hummocks of *Artemisia schmidtiana* 'Nana' provide a lovely link between the

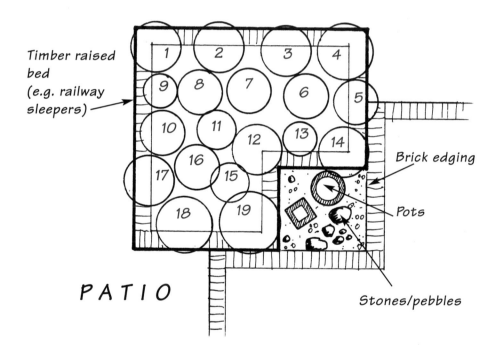

Timber raised bed (e.g. railway sleepers)

Brick edging

Pots

Stones/pebbles

PATIO

planting key

1 *Diascia barberae* 'Blackthorn Apricot'
2 *Campanula carpatica* 'Chewton Joy'
3 *Phlox subulata* 'Bonita'
4 *Artemisia schmidtiana* 'Nana'
5 *Achillea lewisii* 'King Edward'
6 *Rhododendron* 'Palestrina' (evergreen azalea)

7 *Delphinium grandiflorum* 'Blue Butterfly'
8 *Chamaecyparis lawsoniana* 'Gimbornii'
9 *Iris* 'Amber Queen'
10 *Crepis incana*
11 *Linum narbonense*
12 *Pulsatilla vulgaris* 'Barton's Pink'

13 *Helianthemum* 'Wisley White'
14 *Hebe pimeleoides* 'Quicksilver'
15 *Veronica spicata* 'Heidekind'
16 *Calluna vulgaris* 'H.E. Beale'
17 *Viola* 'Maggie Mott'
18 *Helianthemum* 'Wisley Primrose'
19 *Acaena saccaticupula* 'Blue Haze'

pale violet flowers and green foliage of *Phlox subulata* 'Bonita' on one side and the sulphur-yellow heads of the dwarf *Achillea lewisii* 'King Edward' on the other and complement the tiny blue-grey leaves and narrow black stems of *Hebe pimeleoides* 'Quicksilver'. Soft pinks are essential, and there are the long-flowering spikes of *Veronica spicata* 'Heidekind', the exotic-looking,

balloon-like heads of *Pulsatilla vulgaris* 'Barton's Pink' (pasqueflower) and the delicious orange-pink of *Diascia barberae* 'Blackthorn Apricot' and the miniature pink dandelion-like heads of the rosette-forming *Crepis incana*. Complementing these are the equally important blues, provided by the low hummocks and tiny bellflowers of *Campanula carpatica* 'Chewton Joy', by *Linum narbonense* (flax) and by the profusion of bright, delicate trumpets and finely cut foliage of the dwarf *Delphinium grandiflorum* 'Blue Butterfly'.

Artemisia schmidtiana 'Nana' is an excellent, low, edging plant for a raised bed or any well-drained sunny border, particularly if mulched with gravel.

Providing Special Conditions

Raised beds, because they are self-contained, offer you the opportunity to grow plants in conditions that they might otherwise find difficult; this is possible because you are able to control the type of growing medium in the bed. For example, one of the best uses for a raised bed in this respect is for growing ericaceous plants – that is, those that require acid soil – in an area where the natural underlying soil is alkaline. This group of plants includes rhododendrons, azaleas, camellias, and winter- and summer-flowering heathers (*Calluna* and *Erica* species). It is merely a matter of obtaining a suitable acidic soil or compost to fill the bed.

An average-quality topsoil in a raised bed tends to be free-draining and is, therefore, good for alpines and dwarf conifers, although it is too dry for moisture-loving plants such as astilbes and hostas. It is, however, possible, to adapt a raised bed to suit these plants by laying a sheet

of perforated, heavy-duty polythene at the bottom and up the sides of the bed, and then to backfill with a heavier soil, enriched with plenty of organic matter. A thick mulch of bark on top after planting will help conserve moisture, even in dry spells.

other ideas

SINGLE-COLOUR RAISED BED

Adjusting the plant choices can change the gentle and relaxing mood produced by the pastel shades. Use plants with only blue flowers, for example, to create a cooler, more distant effect. The phlox, diascia and achillea could be replaced by *Phlox subulata* 'Oakington Blue Eyes', *Lithodora diffusa* 'Heavenly Blue' and *Aubrieta* 'Triumphante'. The evergreen azalea *Rhododendron* 'Blue Danube', the standard dwarf bearded *Iris* 'Tinkerbell' and *Sisyrinchium idahoense* could replace the white azalea, dwarf bearded iris and *Crepis incana* (pink dandelion). Use *Campanula carpatica* var. *turbinata* 'Karl Foerster' instead of the pink pasqueflower and *Veronica prostrata* (prostrate speedwell) instead of *V. spicata* 'Heidekind'. Finally, replace the pink calluna and yellow helianthemum with *Aster novi-belgii* 'Lady in Blue' and *Geranium wallichianum* 'Buxton's Variety'.

For a more vivid, eye-catching display, add a few hot spots. *Helianthemum* 'Henfield Brilliant' could replace *H.* 'Wisley White', while *H.* 'Old Gold' could replace the diascia. Deep red *Aubrieta* 'Red Carpet' instead of the achillea, *Penstemon pinifolius* 'Mersea Yellow' instead of the pansy and the rose-pink *Phlox subulata* 'McDaniel's Cushion' instead of *P. subulata* 'Bonita' would achieve the desired effect. To finish, use the gold foliage of *Thymus pulegioides* 'Bertram Anderson' instead of the grey artemisia and purple-red *Aster novi-belgii* 'Dandy' in place of *Acaena saccaticupula* 'Blue Haze'.

Formal Beds

Formal gardens rely on a balance of symmetry for their success – repetition and strong, crisp lines of paving and planting. They are usually strongly geometric, using perfect squares, rectangles and circles rather than informal, flowing lines. Often, the most striking examples of formality require all the plants to be carefully shaped and controlled by frequent, regular pruning and trimming.

The modest, formal bed shown overleaf, which measures about 3x3m (10x10ft) and is set in the centre of a lawn, relies more on its precise, geometric shape, enclosed by a ground pattern of old paving bricks, than on the fastidious control of every plant with secateurs and shears. It is a simple layout, of four small, hedged squares within the larger square of brick, and is all the more effective for this simplicity. At the centre is a single, upright accent plant, which is in contrast to the low blocks of planting in the smaller squares around it. Within each of these quarters are two triangular groups of plants, almost separated in the centre by a single, third plant, which acts as a lesser accent or focal point. These inner plantings are identical and the whole plan is symmetrical along both axes, so that, whichever way you look at it, one side of the bed will always be a mirror image of the other. The 'hedges' are separated from each other by narrow strips of gravel, through which the main accent plant grows, allowing limited access for essential plant maintenance.

● option 1

Formal Foliage Bed

The design for a formal bed is a development of some of the earliest formal designs, in which foliage colour and plant form were the principal factors and flowers were not considered at all.

Here, there are some flowers, but they are subsidiary elements in the main scheme, which uses foliage to create the various geometric patterns and shapes. Apart from the hard brick edging, the main framework is provided by *Buxus sempervirens* 'Suffruticosa' (box), which is ideal for small-scale formal work because it has a naturally dwarf, bushy habit and needs trimming only once or twice a year. However, if you wanted to create a feature on a larger scale with taller enclosures, the species *B. sempervirens* would be more appropriate, although it would require more frequent clipping than

the slow-growing cultivar. The central feature is a mophead *Laurus nobilis* 'Aurea' (golden bay), which, like the box, can be trimmed occasionally during the growing season in order to keep its symmetrical shape.

The planting within the squares is identical in order to maintain the symmetry of the design. In the centre is the upright, glaucous-leaved *Hosta* 'Krossa Regal', which has spikes of tubular, lavender-coloured flowers in summer. On one side of this is the dark, glossy, purple foliage of *Heuchera micrantha* var. *diversifolia* 'Palace Purple', which is topped by delicate sprays of tiny, white flowers, while on the other side is the bright gold, densely leaved, ornamental form of marjoram, *Origanum vulgare* 'Thumble's Variety', with its pungent herby smell and dense, small heads of tiny white flowers.

feature plant

HEUCHERA MICRANTHA VAR. DIVERSIFOLIA 'PALACE PURPLE'

This low, compact plant is one of the best purple-leaved perennials for general use. Its glossy, heavily veined leaves are a deep bronze-purple above, with redder undersides, and are borne on slender, dark stems. In early to midsummer tiny white flowers, held well above the foliage on slender, arching stems, last for many weeks. In mild winters many leaves are retained, providing additional colour, especially if early dwarf bulbs are planted nearby.

On good, well-drained, humus-rich soils they will do well in a sunny border. They also thrive in partial shade. An excellent feature plant in mixed and herbaceous borders, they make good ground-cover, especially in groups of three or more next to contrasting plants, such as the silver-leaved deadnettle *Lamium maculatum* 'Beacon Silver'. To keep plants at their best, divide and replant every three or four years. Make sure that the bare, woody stems are buried.

Type of plant: perennial
Height/spread: 45/45cm (18/18in)
Flowering season: early to midsummer
Flower: tiny white flowers on slender stems
Foliage: toothed, dark, glossy, purple-bronze
Position: full sun or light shade
Soil: any well-drained soil
Uses: mixed and herbaceous borders, groundcover, flower arranging
Hardiness: hardy

Small standard tree or shrub

Brick edging

Gravel mulch around planting

Dwarf hedge

Gravel

LAWN

LAWN

planting key

1 *Laurus nobilis* 'Aurea'
2 *Buxus sempervirens* 'Suffruticosa'
3 *Hosta* 'Krossa Regal'
4 *Heuchera micrantha* var. *diversifolia* 'Palace Purple'
5 *Origanum vulgare* 'Thumble's Variety'

• option 2

Formal Colour Theme

Although the lines and layout of this variation are still strictly formal, there is a greater degree of softness to the design, largely because there is no regular clipping or trimming involved, apart from a once yearly prune and tidy up. This bed needs a sunny open position to suit the planting which is predominantly Mediterranean in origin.

Here the theme is concerned as much with colour as form, with mauve, blue and silver the predominant shades. Central to the design is a standard form of *Wisteria* 'Caroline', with its trailing panicles of sweetly scented, lavender-blue and white flowers in late spring. The framework planting to the four squares is the dwarf *Lavandula angustifolia* 'Hidcote', which is pruned in spring and then left alone to form a soft, silver and dark

blue edging. At the centre of each square is a specimen of *Artemisia* 'Powis Castle', with soft, pungent, silver foliage. This needs to be cut back quite hard in early spring in order to maintain the dense, rounded form that is essential to the design. In a good growing year it might be necessary to give it a second, lighter trim in midsummer.

On one side of the artemisia there is *Agapanthus campanulatus* 'Isis', which has

arching, strap-shaped, dark green leaves and globular heads of blue flowers. On the other is a form of sea holly, *Eryngium bourgatii*, with its silver-veined spiky foliage and heads of silver-blue, thistle-like flowers, which remain attractive for weeks in mid- to late summer.

The brick and gravel paving which surrounds the bed both conserves and reflects the heat to the benefit of all the plants.

LAVANDULA ANGUSTIFOLIA 'HIDCOTE'

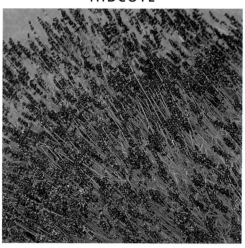

Lavender is well known for its aromatic leaves and scented blue, pink or white flowers. *Lavandula angustifolia* 'Hidcote' makes a neat, dense mound of short, silver-green leaves and long-lasting dark blue flowers in midsummer.

Lavender prefers full sun in any well-drained soil, and it can be used in both formal and informal displays, individually, in groups or as a low hedge or edging. Its scented foliage and flowers are also ideal for cutting and drying. Seed-raised forms of *L. angustifolia* 'Hidcote' can vary so grow from cuttings from the same mother plant if you are planting a hedge. To keep in shape, trim off the flowerheads in late summer or cut plants hard back in early spring.

Common name: lavender
Type of plant: dwarf shrub
Height/spread: 50/50cm (20/20in)
Flowering season: midsummer
Flower: dark blue spikes on narrow stems
Foliage: slender, grey-green leaves
Position: full sun
Soil: any except waterlogged
Uses: mixed borders, formal beds, low hedge, flower arranging
Hardiness: hardy

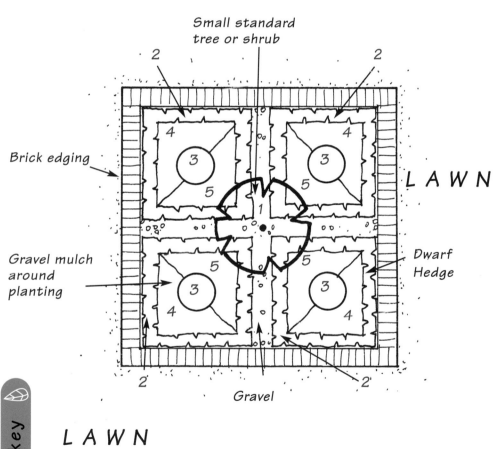

Small standard tree or shrub

Brick edging

Gravel mulch around planting

Dwarf Hedge

LAWN

Gravel

LAWN

planting key

1 *Wisteria* 'Caroline'
2 *Lavandula angustifolia* 'Hidcote'
3 *Artemisia* 'Powis Castle'
4 *Agapanthus campanulatus* 'Isis'
5 *Eryngium bourgatii*

• option 3

Formal Garden in Shade

Buxus species (box), whether the dwarf form or the larger common type is chosen, will grow quite happily in shade and will make a suitable edge for a formal garden or bed in a shady position.

For a brighter effect, however, this design uses the evergreen shrub *Euonymus fortunei* 'Emerald Gaiety', which has small, silver-variegated, grey-green leaves. It makes a slightly looser hedge but, like box, responds well to regular trimming or even the occasional hard pruning if it becomes straggly.

The focal point is a specimen of *Taxus baccata* 'Fastigiata' (fastigiate yew), which naturally makes a tall, slender column, requiring little or no pruning and regrowing readily from old wood if pruned hard in late

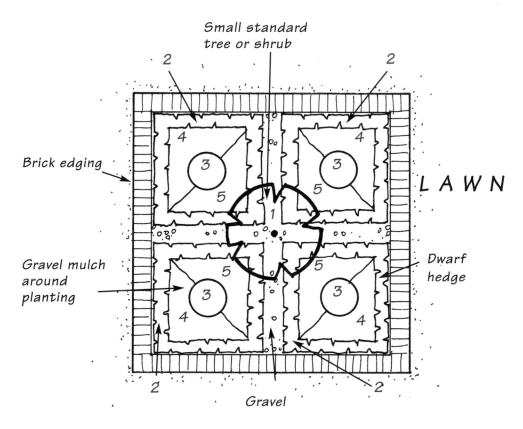

Small standard tree or shrub

Brick edging

Gravel mulch around planting

Dwarf hedge

LAWN

Gravel

LAWN

planting key

1 *Taxus baccata* 'Fastigiata'
2 *Euonymus fortunei* 'Emerald Gaiety'
3 *Lilium regale*
4 *Tiarella cordifolia*
5 *Astilbe arendsii* 'Fanal'

winter or early spring. For a little more colour you could use the golden form, *T. baccata* 'Standishii'.

Within each of the euonymus squares, the central feature is the tall, elegant hardy *Lilium regale* (regal lily), with its

large, pink-tinged, white trumpets in summer standing out against the dark, neat foliage of the yew, and there is a bonus of rich, heavy scent. Around the lilies are blocks of *Tiarella cordifolia* (foam flower), an ideal plant for a shaded or woodland position. Tiarella is a dainty-looking yet durable groundcover perennial with mounds of soft, toothed, pale green leaves and tall slender sprays of tiny, foam-like flowers in spring. On the opposite side, nearest the yew and making a deliberate hot spot, is the taller *Astilbe* × *arendsii* 'Fanal', with its dark green, glossy, deeply cut leaves and upright feathery spikes of tiny dark red flowers in midsummer.

Despite its exotic appearance and rich, heavy scent, *Lilium regale* is surprisingly hardy and reliable.

In addition to their obvious purpose of marking boundaries, hedges can be used as a backdrop to a particular feature, such as a statue, or to subdivide the garden into different spaces.

Neatly clipped hedges have traditionally been grown from conifers, such as × *Cupressocyparis leylandii* (leyland cypress) and *Taxus baccata* (yew), and from *Ligustrum ovalifolium* (privet), *Lonicera nitida* (shrubby honeysuckle) and *Buxus sempervirens* (common box). Many other shrubs, conifers and even trees can be used for the same purpose. *Osmanthus* × *burkwoodii* has tiny, evergreen leaves similar to box but with the bonus of sweetly scented, white flowers in early spring. The holly *Ilex aquifolium* 'Flavescens' makes a superb winter hedge of all gold.

Not all hedges need be formal. If space is available larger shrubs, like *Elaeagnus ebbingei*, which has fragrant winter flowers and silver-green leaves, and *Rosa* 'Pink Grootendorst', with double frilly flowers, make superb features, needing just a good trim to shape them in late winter. Low hedges suit some situations, and here you can use dwarf or slow-growing shrubs. Evergreens, such as *Euonymus fortunei* 'Emerald Gaiety', deciduous plants, with coloured leaves, such as *Berberis thunbergii* 'Atropurpurea Nana', or attractive flowers, such as *Fuchsia* 'Mrs Popple', are worth considering. Finally, for medium-sized and large gardens beech – either plain green *Fagus sylvatica*, or purple *F. sylvatica* Atropurpurea Group – makes a superb hedge, and, though deciduous, is effectively evergreen.

Low-maintenance Formality

One of the essential elements of a traditional formal garden is planting that must be regularly trimmed, pruned and shaped into geometric forms, requiring a good deal of maintenance time and effort. It is, however, possible to achieve a similar effect for much less effort and expenditure of time through careful choice of low-maintenance plants. These either have a naturally formal, dense habit of growth or are less vigorous or slower-growing, thereby needing less frequent trimming or pruning.

Taxus (yew) can need trimming several times a year, but the fastigiate green and gold forms *T. baccata* 'Fastigiata' and 'Standishii' need almost no pruning apart from an annual cutting back to the desired height. The dwarf form of box, *Buxus sempervirens* 'Suffruticosa', is less vigorous than the species. Alternatively, you could use the variegated form, *B. sempervirens* 'Elegantissima', which has slow, dense growth and a naturally

neat shape, for hedging or as an individual specimen. Other dwarf or slow-growing conifers that need little maintenance to keep them looking neat are *Thuja orientalis* 'Aurea Nana', *Juniperus communis* 'Compressa' and *Chamaecyparis lawsoniana* 'Ellwood's Pillar'.

Kitchen Gardens

There is nothing nicer than to be able to pick your own fresh herbs, salads and vegetables and to eat them fresh from the ground. Unfortunately, modern trends mean that many budding gardeners have little spare time for growing food crops in the traditional vegetable plot at the bottom of the garden or in an allotment, and, even when time is available, quite often there just is not enough space.

An excellent compromise is to make a small, ornamental bed for herbs or the kitchen garden to suit both the time and the space you have to spare. Such a bed can be made into a positive design feature and need not, therefore, be tucked away into the far recesses of your plot.

Laying out such a bed in a symmetrical shape, such as a square or, as shown overleaf, a circle, makes it easier and more practicable to fit into most gardens. Choose a size that suits your particular circumstances. This one is about 3m (10ft) in diameter, but you could make it smaller and include fewer plants or larger and extend either the range of produce or the quantity.

The sections are divided by scalloped edging tiles, set to about half their depth directly into the soil. These not only keep the different plant types separate but also provide a permanent visual framework and keep the growing medium separate from its surroundings, which could be lawn, gravel or paving. As in any island bed, the overall effect will be most successful if you keep lower plants at the front, with taller ones behind and in the centre.

• option 1

Culinary Herb Garden

This circular island herb bed or garden serves two purposes. First, it makes a feature in its own right, particularly because of the way the scalloped edging tiles are used to enclose and subdivide the circle. Second, and most obviously, it provides a readily available selection of aromatic and pungent fresh leaves and stems for use in the kitchen.

The evergreen *Rosmarinus officinalis* (rosemary) is a shrub and adds an important element of structure and focus to the display. It does need an occasional trim to keep it within bounds or, when necessary, a much harder prune immediately after its pale blue flowers have gone over in spring.

The bed is relatively low-maintenance, including perennial or woody herbs that need a once- or twice-

yearly trim to keep them fresh and tidy. These include *Melissa officinalis* (lemon balm), which you can cut down to the ground in late winter, and *Allium schoenoprasum* (chives), a plant which naturally dies down at the end of each season. It is a good idea to include one or two shorter-lived herbs that are particularly useful in the kitchen, such as *Petroselinum crispum* (parsley) and *Ocimum basilicum* (basil), which are best grown from seed each spring and will therefore need replacing annually if you wish to keep growing them.

If left to their own devices, all herbs will eventually flower. Some, such as the pink globes of chives in spring are especially attractive, while others, like the tiny greeny-white blooms of *Artemisia dracunculus* (French tarragon), which appear later in summer, are more subtle and of little consequence.

feature plant

MELISSA OFFICINALIS

Originally grown to attract bees to the garden, *Melissa officinalis* is an attractive addition to the herb garden. It occurs naturally throughout southern Europe and into western Asia and northern Africa, and has been cultivated for about 2000 years for its aromatic properties. The small, toothed leaves are light green, and when they are crushed they release a delightful lemon fragrance. Insignificant pale yellow flowers are borne in whorls in summer. You can grow lemon balm in any soil, even poor soil, in sun or shade.

There are two fine cultivars. *M. officinalis* 'All Gold' (**pictured above centre**) has bright yellow foliage and is a fine plant for cheering up shady corners. If it is grown in full sun, the leaves will scorch. *M. officinalis* 'Aurea' is similar to the species, but the leaves are delightfully splashed with yellow.

Common name: bee balm, lemon balm
Type of plant: perennial
Height/spread: 80/45cm (32/18in)
Flowering season: summer
Flower: pale yellow spikes
Foliage: ovate, toothed, light green
Position: full sun
Soil: poor, well-drained
Uses: culinary, edging, herbaceous border
Hardiness: hardy

Gravel/stone chippings

Terracotta scalloped edging tiles

planting key

1 *Rosmarinus officinalis*
2 *Hyssopus officinalis*
3 *Melissa officinalis*
4 *Mentha spicata*
5 *Salvia officinalis*
6 *Artemisia dracunculus*
7 *Petroselinum crispum*
8 *Allium schoenoprasum*
9 *Thymus vulgaris*
10 *Ocimum basilicum*
11 *Origanum vulgare*

• option 2

Ornamental Herb Garden

Placing ordinary, cultivated herbs, such as *Salvia officinalis* (common sage) or *Petroselinum crispum* (parsley), together in a bed will produce a relatively restrained composition in terms of colour: there will be lots of green and silver foliage tones with odd pockets of small white or pink flowers. Many ornamental forms of herbs have evolved from the original wild plants, however, and these can add an extra dimension to a herb garden, making it a more striking feature, yet with the same culinary benefits.

Central to this design is *Laurus nobilis* (bay), which provides an evergreen focal point that is made more prominent by regular trimming into a tall, narrow cone. It provides an excellent dark backdrop to several plants

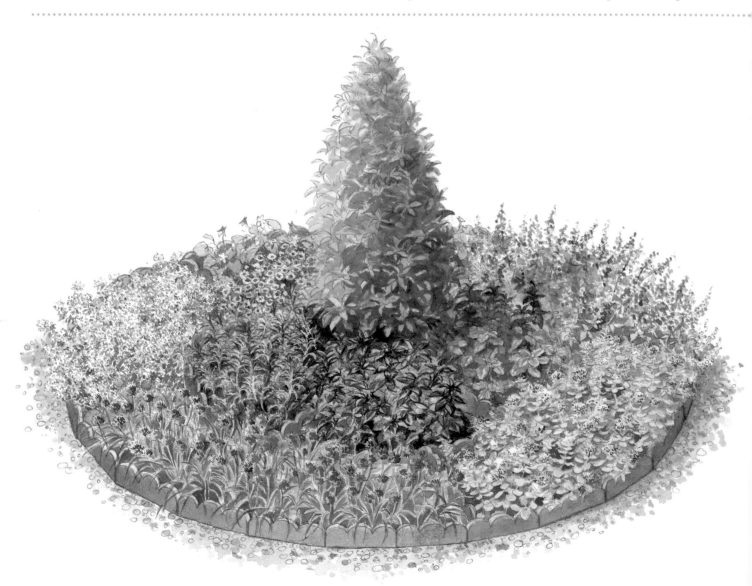

that have been selected for their golden foliage: *Melissa officinalis* 'Aurea' (golden lemon balm), with its citrus smell; the yellow form of feverfew, *Tanacetum parthenium* 'Aureum', which is more pungent; and the golden marjoram, *Origanum vulgare* 'Aureum', which, like the balm, is especially attractive to bees and other beneficial insects. By contrast, there is the soft purple-grey of *Salvia officinalis* 'Purpurascens' and its purple

and white hooded flowers in summer, and the yellow-variegated leaves of *Mentha* × *gentilis* 'Variegata' (ginger mint) with its surprising scent of apples.

Silver or grey foliage is essential in any scheme, but especially in herb plantings. Soft *Artemisia alba* 'Canescens' and familiarly pungent *Nepeta* × *faassenii* (catmint), with its pale blue flowers for many weeks in summer, are grown here more for appearance than culinary use.

feature plant

LAURUS NOBILIS

This handsome evergreen tree or shrub produces the leaves that are an essential part of so many classic dishes and an essential ingredient of bouquet garni. *Laurus nobilis* (bay, bay laurel, sweet bay) is found throughout Mediterranean countries. The dark green, leathery leaves are distinctively aromatic. In spring, clusters of small yellow flowers are borne, followed by small, purplish-black berries.

Bay does best in fairly rich, moist, well-drained soil in a sheltered spot. Although not reliably hardy, in favoured areas it will grow into a large tree. It responds well to pruning, and can be easily trained into various shapes.

Common name: bay, bay laurel, sweet bay
Type of plant: tree
Height/spread: 12/10m (40/33ft)
Flowering season: spring
Flower: clusters of small, yellow-green
Foliage: glossy, dark green
Position: full sun or partial shade
Soil: rich, moist but well-drained
Uses: specimen, topiary, culinary
Hardiness: half-hardy

Gravel/stone chippings

Terracotta scalloped edging tiles

planting key

1 *Laurus nobilis*
2 *Mentha* × *gentilis* 'Variegata'
3 *Melissa officinalis* 'Aurea'
4 *Salvia officinalis* 'Purpurascens'
5 *Artemisia alba* 'Canescens'
6 *Tanacetum parthenium* 'Aureum'
7 *Viola odorata* 'Alba'
8 *Nepeta* × *faassenii*
9 *Origanum vulgare* 'Aureum'
10 *Allium senescens* var. *glaucum*
11 *Thymus vulgaris* 'Silver Posie'

• option 3

Vegetable Garden

A carefully planned and laid-out kitchen garden can be extremely attractive, especially when it is arranged in the form of a circle. The volume of produce may not match that of a conventional plot, but it makes up for it by its appearance and its convenience since it could be located near to the house and used as an ornamental feature.

As in all planting schemes, a degree of structure is vital, and here it is provided by a narrow, columnar, ballerina crabapple, 'Maypole', in the centre of the circle. Around it the blocks of planting use a combination of leaf, stem and fruit to provide contrast and texture. The bright, fresh green of the low-growing asparagus pea nestle tightly between the striking red- and white-stemmed, dark-leaved ruby chard and the bright red fruits and

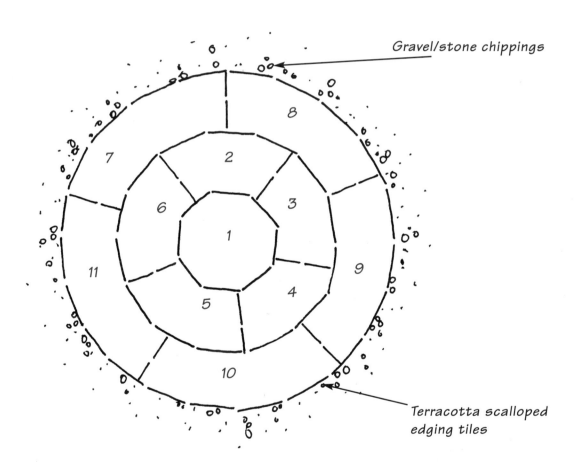

Gravel/stone chippings

Terracotta scalloped edging tiles

1 Ballerina crabapple 'Maypole'
2 Asparagus pea
3 Ruby chard
4 Florence fennel
5 Dwarf French bean
6 Bush tomato
7 Lettuce 'Salad Bowl'
8 Beetroot 'Boltardy'
9 Lettuce 'Valeria Red'
10 Spring onion 'White Lisbon'
11 Perpetual strawberry 'Gento'

yellow-centred flowers of bush tomatoes. Next to these the leafy green and pendulous pods of dwarf French beans contrast with the finely cut, aniseed-scented foliage of Florence fennel, with

Around the outer edge are more colour and textural contrasts. The neat green leafiness of the lettuce 'Salad Bowl' is next to the dark rich ruby of beetroot 'Boltardy' and its glossy, purple-red veined leaves. The green-tinged, coppery-red of lettuce 'Valeria Red' is in marked contrast to the upright, narrow white and green stems of spring onion 'White Lisbon', and the yellow-centred white flowers and sweet, bright red fruits of the perpetual strawberry 'Gento' creep over the tiled edging.

its greenish-white bulbous stems.

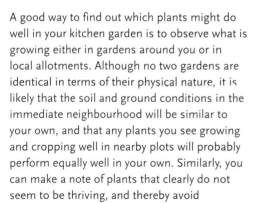

The bright red stems and glossy leaves of ruby chard make a striking conbination for kitchen and ornamental gardens.

Plants by Observation

A good way to find out which plants might do well in your kitchen garden is to observe what is growing either in gardens around you or in local allotments. Although no two gardens are identical in terms of their physical nature, it is likely that the soil and ground conditions in the immediate neighbourhood will be similar to your own, and that any plants you see growing and cropping well in nearby plots will probably perform equally well in your own. Similarly, you can make a note of plants that clearly do not seem to be thriving, and thereby avoid including them in your own design.

Observation of this nature will give you an opportunity to see how large or vigorous certain plants may be, when they are growing in your locality; this will enable you to avoid selecting ones that may be quite unsuitable for the location you have in mind for them because of their rate of growth and eventual size.

This principle does not only apply to the vegetable garden – it is also a useful ploy when planning the ornamental planting throughout your garden as a whole. Remember to observe neighbouring gardens at all times of the year, not just in hte height of summer, so that you will be able to appreciate all the options open to you, thus widening your choice.

FRAGARIA ANANASSA 'GENTO'

Perpetual-fruiting, also known as remontant, strawberries produce fruit in flushes throughout summer, stopping only when the first frosts occur. If you have some cloches, it is possible to extend the fruiting season by covering plants in early autumn. Strawberries can be grown in the smallest of gardens and will produce a good crop of fruit even when grown in a container on the patio. They need rich soil to produce a continuous supply of fruits, and they need a position in full sun.

Replace plants from new runners every year or the size and weight of the fruit will deteriorate in the second and subsequent years.

Common name: perpetual strawberry
Type of plant: perennial
Height/spread: 20/50cm (8/20in)
Flowering season: late spring
Flower: five-petalled, white
Foliage: bright green, three-lobed, toothed
Position: full sun or light shade
Soil: rich, moist but well-drained
Uses: fruit
Hardiness: hardy

Garden Designs

Gardens do not always fall neatly into the category of a back garden with an area of lawn and beds and borders. Many home-owners also have a front garden, which is more visible to passers-by and visitors than the area at the back. Other gardens are built on slopes or have extended patios, and in towns many people have a courtyard to turn into their ideal garden.

Small Front Gardens

Most front gardens have a different role from back gardens. They are chiefly concerned with appearance and providing an attractive, living framework to a house or apartment for both the owner and visitors. Back gardens, on the other hand, not only have to be attractive but must also fulfill a number of other functions, such as providing areas for play, relaxation and entertaining.

The example shown overleaf is quite modest in size, about 5x5m (16x16ft), and typical of today's smaller gardens. A circular design, based on a ring of bricks inset with gravel, is a successful way of disguising the squareness of the plot. Equally effective is the brick path from the pavement to the front door. Rather than following a simple straight line up the centre of the garden, it begins in one corner and meanders across the circle and through a central island bed of low planting. The bricks are laid end to end (in the style known as stretcher bond) parallel to the edges of the path, which accentuates its long, sinuous shape.

The planting around the perimeter of the garden is mulched with gravel to match the gravel within the circle, so that it blends and softens any hard edges. At the sides of the porch planting wraps around the front and helps to frame the front door. Troughs of annuals and bulbs beneath the windows provide splashes of seasonal colour but do not interfere with the practicalities of cleaning. As a final touch, there is a small tree in the corner next to the road to act as a focal point and to bring some vertical interest and a little bit of privacy.

• option 1

Low-maintenance Front Garden

A front garden will create an attractive setting for a house or apartment, but it need not be functional in the way that a back garden must be, because you are unlikely to spend much time in it.

If time for gardening is limited, a low-maintenance garden at the front is likely to be desirable so you can concentrate on the back garden. Evergreens are always valuable, with their ability to suppress weeds and cover bare soil. Large plants, such as the holly *Ilex aquifolium* 'Silver Milkmaid' and *Viburnum tinus* 'Variegatum', are good for adding height and a framework. In contrast, low-growing evergreens, such as grey-green *Juniperus horizontalis* 'Hughes', form carpets of attractive foliage.

Not all evergreens rely solely on foliage for interest. Heathers especially have a valuable, long-flowering

period. This design includes the golden *Calluna vulgaris* 'Robert Chapman', which has soft purple late-summer flowers, and *Erica darleyensis* 'Darley Dale', with pink flowers in late winter.

Ornamental grasses make excellent accent plants. *Miscanthus sinensis* 'Gracillimus' has soft flowering plumes in late summer, and *Panicum virgatum* 'Rubrum' has blue-green leaves, red-purple in autumn, and tiny seedheads.

Perennials make good groundcover too, and this scheme includes the dwarf, purple-red Michaelmas daisy *Aster novi-belgii* 'Dandy' and the taller daylily *Hemerocallis* 'Burning Daylight'.

Hydrangea arborescens 'Annabelle', although deciduous, makes a superb clump of leaves, topped by giant, white flowers. *Hypericum* 'Hidcote Variegated', another clump-former, has silver-edged leaves and flowers for weeks in summer.

feature plant

CHOISYA TERNATA

This medium to large evergreen shrub, despite its rather soft, exotic appearance, is surprisingly hardy in a sheltered position. It forms a dense mound of glossy, green, divided leaves, which are quite pungent when crushed. Clusters of sweetly scented white flowers appear in spring over many weeks. Occasionally, a second flush of flowers emerges towards the end of summer.

In addition to its attractive flowers, it is an excellent green foil for other plants, and thrives in a range of positions, from full sun to quite heavy shade (flowering is less dramatic here). Excellent as taller groundcover and for cut flowers, it tolerates most soils, even quite alkaline, dry ones, but like most evergreens it must have good drainage. To keep it in shape, prune lightly immediately after flowering.

Common name: Mexican orange blossom
Type of plant: shrub
Height/spread: 1.8/1.8m (6/6ft) or more
Flowering season: late spring, occasionally late summer
Flower: clusters of white, scented blooms
Foliage: finger-like, glossy dark green
Position: full sun to medium or heavy shade
Soil: any if well-drained
Uses: specimen, wall shrub, backdrop, groundcover, cut flower
Hardiness: hardy

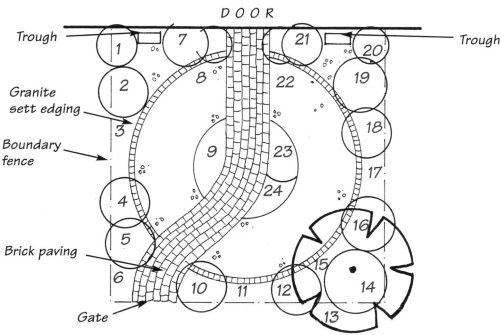

Trough — Granite sett edging — Boundary fence — Brick paving — Gate — DOOR — Trough

planting key

1 *Miscanthus sinensis* 'Gracillimus'
2 *Prunus laurocerasus* 'Otto Luyken'
3 *Aster novi-belgii* 'Dandy'
4 *Hemerocallis* 'Burning Daylight'
5 *Ilex aquifolium* 'Silver Milkmaid'
6 *Matteuccia struthiopteris*
7 *Viburnum tinus* 'Variegatum'
8 *Euphorbia amygdaloides* 'Purpurea'
9 *Erica vagans* 'Saint Keverne'
10 *Thuja occidentalis* 'Rheingold'
11 *Astilbe* 'Sprite'
12 *Buxus sempervirens* 'Elegantissima'

13 *Malus* 'Evereste'
14 *Hydrangea arborescens* 'Annabelle'
15 *Heuchera* 'Rachel'
16 *Choisya ternata* 'Sundance'
17 *Perovskia* 'Blue Spire'
18 *Anemone* × *hybrida* 'Richard Ahrens'
19 *Potentilla fruticosa* 'Abbotswood'
20 *Panicum virgatum* 'Rubrum'
21 *Hypericum* 'Hidcote Variegated'
22 *Juniperus horizontalis* 'Hughes'
23 *Erica darleyensis* 'Darley Dale'
24 *Calluna vulgaris* 'Robert Chapman'

Foliage Front Garden

The range of foliage colour, shape, size and texture found in plants is so great that it is quite possible to design a complete garden around foliage plants.

In such a scheme, flowers that do appear are almost irrelevant. Even in this small garden there is a huge variety. There are the large, gold-edged, heart-shaped leaves of *Hosta fortunei* var. *aureomarginata* and the even more dramatic blue-grey, jagged-edged *Acanthus mollis* (bear's breeches), which also has bold, upright spikes of green and purple flowers. In strong contrast is the soft, feathery, grey texture and pungent aroma of *Artemisia stelleriana* 'Boughton Silver' set against the horse chestnut-like leaves of the perennial *Rodgersia aesculifolia*. Vertical emphasis is provided by the narrow spikiness of *Iris pallida* 'Variegata' – the blue-green leaves are edged

with gold and topped with blue flowers in late spring – and the long, narrow, silver-edged leaves of the grass *Miscanthus sinensis* 'Variegatus'.

Evergreen and deciduous shrubs make a permanent framework. There are the winter gold of *Ilex aquifolium* 'Flavescens' (moonlight holly) and the soft purple masses of *Cotinus coggygria* Rubrifolius Group, which is topped with a misty smoke of minute flowers in summer.

Variations in size and scale add extra interest. The tiny variegated leaves and low creeping habit of *Cotoneaster atropurpureus* 'Variegatus' contrast with the massive, upright, sword-shaped evergreen foliage of *Phormium tenax* Purpureum Group, and the small, neat gold-coloured spears of *Spiraea japonica* 'Golden Princess' contrast with the large, walnut-like foliage of *Koelreuteria paniculata* (golden rain tree).

feature plant

ALCHEMILLA MOLLIS

Alchemilla mollis (lady's mantle) has soft, pale green, rounded leaves that form a gentle, dense mound of foliage in most soils in full sun or medium shade. In summer the foliage is almost hidden by frothy panicles of tiny yellow-green flowers, which remain attractive even when they are dead. Both the leaves and flowers can be cut for arranging. Every few years, lift the plant in early spring and split off pieces from the edge for replanting, discarding the central crown. Alternatively, you should find plenty of self-sown seedlings, which can be replanted directly, or potted on until big enough to plant out.

Common name: lady's mantle
Type of plant: hardy perennial
Height/spread: 45/60cm (18/24in)
Flowering season: early to late summer
Flower: tiny, yellow-green, forming frothy sprays
Foliage: round, wavy-edged, pale green
Position: full sun to semi-shade
Soil: most, except extremes of wet and dry
Uses: edging, groundcover, foil to other plants, flower arranging
Hardiness: hardy

Plan labels

DOOR

Trough

Trough

Granite sett edging

Boundary fence

Brick paving

Gate

planting key

1 *Spiraea japonica* 'Golden Princess'
2 *Phormium tenax* Purpureum Group
3 *Rodgersia aesculifolia*
4 *Artemisia stelleriana* 'Boughton Silver'
5 *Ilex aquifolium* 'Flavescens'
6 *Asplenium scolopendrium*
7 *Pittosporum* 'Garnettii'
8 *Viburnum davidii*
9 *Liriope spicata* 'Alba'
10 *Taxus baccata* 'Fastigiata'
11 *Iris pallida* 'Variegata'
12 *Berberis media* 'Red Jewel'
13 *Koelreuteria paniculata*
14 *Cotinus coggygria* Rubrifolius Group
15 *Hosta fortunei* var. *aureomarginata*
16 *Physocarpus opulifolius* 'Dart's Gold'
17 *Alchemilla mollis*
18 *Salix lanata*
19 *Photinia fraseri* 'Rubens'
20 *Miscanthus sinensis* 'Variegatus'
21 *Acanthus mollis*
22 *Cotoneaster atropurpureus* 'Variegatus'
23 *Heuchera* 'Chocolate Ruffles'
24 *Campanula garganica* 'Dickson's Gold'

• **option 3**

Cottage-garden-style Front Garden

The design for this small garden has deliberately focused on summer interest, with the emphasis on flowering perennials and climbers.

Even this style of garden will benefit from the inclusion of a number of plants with a woody framework, not least of which are the *Magnolia stellata* (star magnolia), which makes a spectacular focal point at the entrance to

the garden and the *Laburnum* x *watereri* 'Vossii' in the othr corner, with its masses of pendent yellow flowers in late spring. Lilacs are ideal in cottage gardens, but in this limited space the dwarf form *Syringa meyeri* var. *spontanea* 'Palibin' is used. It is much neater and smaller than the species, although the flowers are just as fragrant.

Scented flowers are an essential element of this style

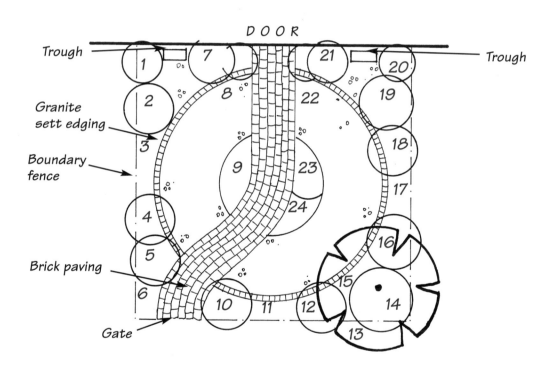

1 *Alcea rosea* Chater's Double Group
2 *Rosa* 'Graham Thomas'
3 *Phlox paniculata* 'Prince of Orange'
4 *Paeonia lactiflora* 'Sarah Bernhardt'
5 *Magnolia stellata*
6 *Astilbe arendsii* 'Federsee'
7 *Philadelphus* 'Manteau d'Hermine'

8 *Aster thomsonii* 'Nanus'
9 *Achillea* 'Apfelblüte'
10 *Weigela florida* 'Foliis Purpureis'
11 *Geranium* x *oxonianum* 'Wargrave Pink'
12 *Euphorbia griffithii* 'Fireglow'
13 *Laburnum* x *watereri* 'Vossii'
14 *Syringa meyeri* var. *spontanea* 'Palibin'
15 *Dicentra* 'Pearl Drops'
16 *Spiraea* 'Arguta'

17 *Crocosmia* x *crocosmiiflora* 'Emily McKenzie'
18 *Ceratostigma willmottianum*
19 *Rosa* 'Buff Beauty'
20 *Phlox paniculata* 'Eva Cullum'
21 *Jasminum nudiflorum* 'Aureum'
22 *Papaver orientale* 'Black and White'
23 *Agapanthus* Headbourne hybrids
24 *Aquilegia vulgaris* 'White Bonnets'

of planting, and both the modestly growing *Philadelphus* 'Manteau d'Hermine' and the lovely double pink *Paeonia lactiflora* 'Sarah Bernhardt' provide plenty of fragrance early in the summer. Later in the year the shrub roses *Rosa* 'Graham Thomas' and *R.* 'Buff Beauty' provide more scent.

Traditional cottage-garden perennials have been carefully chosen to give good

value for money. They need no staking and have a long flowering period. In addition, there are contrasts in foliage and form to create some satisfying plant associations – the fiery orange spikes and stiff, narrow foliage of *Crocosmia* x *crocosmiiflora* 'Emily McKenzie' (montbretia) are set against the twiggy, greeny-grey leaves and fluffy blue flowers of *Ceratostigma willmottianum*; and the delicate, blue-grey, finely cut leaves and cream, heart-shaped flowers of *Dicentra* 'Pearl Drops' nestle against the dense, bright green, leafy mounds and silver-pink flowers of *Geranium* x *oxonianum* 'Wargrave Pink'.

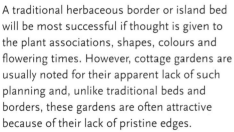

Agapanthus Headbourne hybrids is one of the most reliable, unfussy perennials for a sunny border or a large container.

other ideas

COLOUR-THEMED COTTAGE-GARDEN PLANTING

The selection of flowering plants will provide a cheerful mix of colours throughout summer. You could, however, change the mood relatively easily by replacing the vibrant, 'hotter' reds and oranges with softer, pastel shades and tones. *Phlox paniculata* 'Prince of Orange' could make way for *P. maculata* 'Omega', which has pink-centred, white flowers, while the long-flowering *Campanula persicifolia* 'Telham Beauty' would make a good blue alternative to the red-orange tones of the euphorbia. Cream or pale yellow flowers, such as *Kniphofia* 'Little Maid' would make a good substitute for the crocosmia, and you could swap the golden flowers of the laburnum with the more delicate white, scented blooms of *Malus hupehensis*.

In a heavy soil in light shade replace the agapanthus and ceratostigma with *Iris foetidissima* (stinking gladwyn) and *Geranium phaeum*. Hardy anemones, such as *A. hybrida* 'Königin Charlotte' (**pictured above**) or the white-flowered *A. hybrida* 'Andrea Atkinson', would be good substitutes for the achillea and *Papaver orientale* 'Black and White'. *Digitalis* species (foxglove) would be more suitable than *Alcea* species (hollyhock), and the roses could be replaced with hydrangeas, such as *H.* 'Preziosa' and *H. aspera* Villosa Group, which will provide foliage interest too. Finally, swap the aster with the more shade-tolerant, blue-flowered *Geranium sylvaticum* 'Mayflower'.

Planting for a Cottage-garden Effect

A traditional herbaceous border or island bed will be most successful if thought is given to the plant associations, shapes, colours and flowering times. However, cottage gardens are usually noted for their apparent lack of such planning and, unlike traditional beds and borders, these gardens are often attractive because of their lack of pristine edges.

A woody backbone of shrubby plants and climbers, including roses, jasmine, *Syringa* (lilac), philadelphus and clematis, should provide a framework for a mixed planting of perennials. Rather than being planted in blocks, they should be mixed with tall plants such as *Alcea* (hollyhock), *Digitalis* (foxglove) and *Verbascum* (mullein) interspersed at irregular intervals, relieving flatness. Perennials that self-seed, such as *Alchemilla* (lady's mantle) and *Centranthus* (valerian), should be allowed to renew themselves.

Paving needs to be the sort that plants can grow through – gravel or stone chippings; old bricks laid without mortar on a bed of sand; or natural flagstones with joints filled with sand or grit and laid on sand directly on top of the soil. All can be softened with low perennials.

Sloping Gardens

Few gardens are exactly level, although relatively minor slopes of, say, 1 in 25 or less can be easily accommodated with an occasional slight change of level, such as from a patio down one or two fairly shallow steps to the lawn. There are, however, gardens where such modest changes are not feasible because the ground slopes so much that it is almost impossible to create any garden feature. Gardens with steep slopes will, therefore, need to be terraced by cutting into the slope horizontally, or nearly so, to create relatively level areas large enough to accommodate a patio or pond. The process of terracing, however, leaves a vertical face or 'cliff' of soil at the back of the level area, and this will quickly become unstable. The solution is to build a rigid horizontal support or retaining wall, which can be made from any strong, durable material, such as brick, stone, concrete or even heavy, treated pieces of wood.

In the example shown overleaf, coursed limestone walling has been used to build retaining walls, which support a lawn at the highest level above a lower patio. Rather than having a straight flight of steps from bottom to top, the feature has been made more attractive by introducing a narrow, intermediate level or 'landing' with generous planting, and the steps are divided into two flights, which are offset to provide changes of direction and view. The walls and steps provide a strong horizontal emphasis, which is counterbalanced by the introduction of an arch across each flight of steps and by the careful selection of plants to hang over the edges of the walls to soften them.

• option 1

Hot, Dry Sloping Garden

When you modify a sloping garden by terracing it with retaining walls into a series of level areas, you create a series of raised beds, one above the other. One of the by-products is that the drainage in the 'raised beds' is usually improved. If these terraces face the prevailing sun, the outcome is hot, dry soil.

Many plants not only tolerate but actually prefer these conditions. This scheme includes *Osteospermum ecklonis*, which trails over walls and has an almost non-stop succession of large, pale violet daisies with a dark eye. Equally at home in this environment and also excellent for trailing is the rock rose *Helianthemum* 'Henfield Brilliant', which has grey foliage and rose-like, scarlet-

orange flowers. Many evergreens require good drainage and will make a valuable contribution here. Suggestions include *Hebe* 'Marjorie', a neat mound which has masses of violet and white flowers, *Elaeagnus pungens* 'Dicksonii', with leathery, silver-green leaves splashed gold, and *Juniperus horizontalis* 'Blue Chip', another good edging plant, which forms a dense carpet of steel blue foliage.

In contrast to the trailing and weeping plants, the arches are planted with scented climbers to add a vertical dimension. *Jasminum officinale* 'Fiona Sunrise' makes a bright splash of gold and has clusters of white flowers, and *Lonicera japonica* var. *repens* has dark green, red-tinged foliage and small but very effective red and cream flowers for weeks during summer.

feature plant

YUCCA FILAMENTOSA

Yuccas are among the most striking plants that you can grow, and they thrive in hot, dry sites. Their bold clumps of dark foliage make them excellent for growing as individual architectural specimens, but they can also be used as a backdrop or foil for other, contrasting plants. *Y. filamentosa* produces tufts of evergreen leaves edged with yellow and thin filaments, as well as attractive white flowers in the latter part of the season, giving prolonged interest to summer displays in beds and borders. It can be grown successfully in a large container in a sunny place. It is not as reliably hardy as some of the other yuccas, however, so if your garden is prone to frost make sure it is grown in a sheltered spot.

Common name: Spanish dagger
Type of plant: shrub
Height/spread: 1.8/1.8m (6/6ft)
Flowering season: late summer to autumn
Flower: panicles of white, bell-shaped blooms
Foliage: stiff, pointed, arching, blue- to dark green
Position: full sun
Soil: any if well-drained
Uses: specimen
Hardiness: hardy to −5°C (23°F)

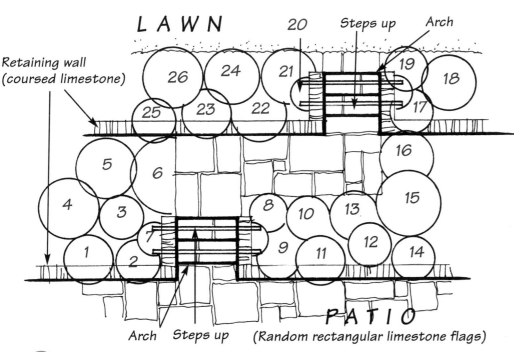

planting key

1 *Osteospermum ecklonis*
2 *Cotoneaster dammeri*
3 *Lotus hirsutus*
4 *Yucca gloriosa*
5 *Elaeagnus pungens* 'Dicksonii'
6 *Ceratostigma plumbaginoides*
7 *Jasminum officinale* 'Fiona Sunrise'
8 *Stipa arundinacea*
9 *Helianthemum* 'Henfield Brilliant'
10 *Berberis thunbergii* 'Silver Beauty'
11 *Juniperus horizontalis* 'Blue Chip'
12 *Rosa* 'Nozomi'
13 *Ajuga reptans* 'Variegata'
14 *Anthemis punctata* subsp. *cupaniana*
15 *Hebe* 'Marjorie'
16 *Lavandula stoechas* subsp. *pedunculata*
17 *Genista lydia*
18 *Euphorbia characias* 'Goldbrook'
19 *Fuchsia* 'Lady Thumb'
20 *Lonicera japonica* var. *repens*
21 *Teucrium chamaedrys*
22 *Gypsophila repens* 'Rosea'
23 *Convolvulus cneorum*
24 *Iris* 'Frost and Flame'
25 *Hedera helix* 'Glacier'
26 *Caryopteris clandonensis* 'Worcester Gold'

• option 2

Sloping Garden with 'Cool' Colour Scheme

Colour in a garden can be used in several ways. By choosing colours from different parts of the spectrum and in varying intensities it is possible to create a specific mood or atmosphere.

Bright reds, hot orange, and rich, sunflower yellows will generate feelings of warmth and liveliness. Blues, white, and lemon- or primrose-yellow, however, alter the mood to one of cool calm, creating the perfect place to relax. Here, the edges of the terraces are softened by low,

prostrate and trailing plants. Some, such as the evergreen dwarf conifers *Tsuga canadensis* 'Pendula' and *Juniperus sabina* 'Tamariscifolia', provide a year-round framework. Others, like *Lithodora diffusa* 'Heavenly Blue' and the white-flowered alpine *Phlox subulata* 'Maischnee', give splashes of colour against the foliage.

Further structure and height come from the evergreen *Pittosporum tenuifolium*

'Irene Paterson', and the long-flowering *Potentilla fruticosa* 'Primrose Beauty'. Silvers and greys are good foils for other colours; here they are found in *Achillea* 'Moonshine', *Cerastium tomentosum* var. *columnae*, *Campanula persicifolia* 'Hampstead White', and the blue-flowered *Iris pallida* 'Argentea Variegata', which is set against the silver of *Teucrium fruticans* (shrubby germander).

other ideas

TERRACE GARDEN WITH 'HOT' COLOUR THEME

The cool colour theme illustrated relies for effect on blues, pale yellows, white, and silver or grey. However, many of the plants suggested have warm or vibrant forms – for example, the sulphur-yellow *Achillea* 'Moonshine' could be replaced by the rosy-pink *A. millefolium* 'Cerise Queen'; the pale blue iris could be replaced by the deep yellow *Iris* 'Berkeley Gold'; and the purple-pink *Clematis alpina* 'Ruby' could replace *C. alpina* 'Frances Rivis'.

Other simple changes could be the bright red *Potentilla fruticosa* 'Red Ace' for the pale lemon, grey-leaved *P. fruticosa* 'Primrose Beauty'; the deep red-pink *Hemerocallis* 'Cherry Cheeks' for *H. citrina*; the climbing red-flowered *Rosa* 'Paul's Scarlet Climber' for its yellow equivalent; and the deep crimson alpine *Phlox subulata* 'Red Wings' instead of its white equivalent, *P. subulata* 'Maischnee'.

Purple- or pink-toned foliage add to the effect. Replace the hebe with the cream-splashed, purple leaves of *Berberis thunbergii* 'Rose Glow' and the blue *Hosta sieboldiana* var. *elegans* with the purple leaves and coral pink flowers of *Heuchera* 'Rachel'. Create some real hot spots with flame-orange *Crocosmia* 'Lucifer' (**pictured above**) and deep yellow *Rudbeckia fulgida* var. *sullivantii* 'Goldsturm' instead of *Hosta undulata* var. *albomarginata* and the helictotrichon.

LAWN 20 Steps up Arch

Retaining wall (coursed limestone)

26 24 21 19 18
25 23 22 17
5 6 16
4 3 8 15
7 10 13
1 9 12 14
2 11

Arch Steps up (Random rectangular limestone flags)

PATIO

planting key

1 *Veronica spicata* subsp. *incana* 'Silver Carpet'
2 *Hedera helix* 'Ivalace'
3 *Achillea* 'Moonshine'
4 *Iris pallida* 'Argentea Variegata'
5 *Teucrium fruticans*
6 *Vinca minor* 'La Grave'
7 *Clematis alpina* 'Frances Rivis'
8 *Helictotrichon sempervirens*
9 *Tsuga canadensis* 'Pendula'
10 *Potentilla fruticosa* 'Primrose Beauty'
11 *Genista pilosa*
12 *Lithodora diffusa* 'Heavenly Blue'

13 *Hosta undulata* var. *albomarginata*
14 *Phlox subulata* 'Maischnee'
15 *Pittosporum tenuifolium* 'Irene Paterson'
16 *Hemerocallis citrina*
17 *Campanula* 'Birch Hybrid'
18 *Hebe* 'Bowles's Hybrid'
19 *Viola riviniana* Purpurea Group
20 *Rosa* 'Paul's Lemon Pillar'
21 *Hosta sieboldiana* var. *elegans*
22 *Juniperus sabina* 'Tamariscifolia'
23 *Cerastium tomentosum* var. *columnae*
24 *Campanula persicifolia* 'Hampstead White'
25 *Aurinia saxatilis* 'Citrina'
26 *Viburnum tinus* 'Eve Price'

• **option 3**
Sloping Terrace Garden **in Shade**

Variations in the amount of sun falling on different parts of your garden will call for different approaches in your choice of plants for those areas. Where there is little or no sun, such as on this shady, terraced slope, plants have been chosen that will not just survive in such conditions but will actually thrive because they do not appreciate hot, direct sun.

Typical of such plants are the beautiful evergreen azalea *Rhododendron* 'Vuyk's Rosyred' and *Pieris japonica* 'Variegata', both of which are much happier in a sheltered semi-woodland situation. More evergreen structural planting is provided by the bold-leaved *Aucuba japonica* 'Picturata' and the prostrate golden yew, *Taxus baccata* 'Repens Aurea'. A particular highlight is the slow-growing maple *Acer shirasawanum*

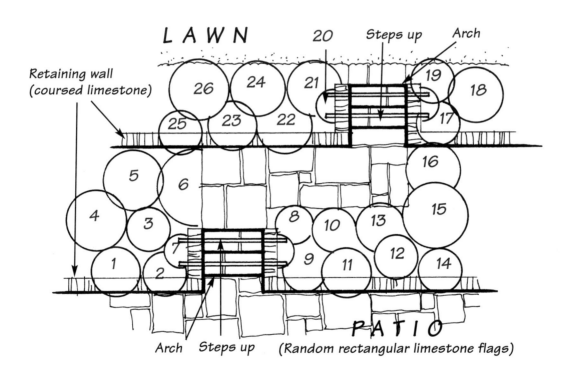

planting key

1 *Vinca minor* 'Argentovariegata'
2 *Taxus baccata* 'Repens Aurea'
3 *Rhododendron* 'Vuyk's Rosyred' (evergreen azalea)
4 *Acer shirasawanum* 'Aureum'
5 *Choisya* 'Aztec Pearl'
6 *Astilbe* 'Willie Buchanan'
7 *Clematis* 'Nelly Moser'
8 *Geranium phaeum* 'Album'
9 *Polystichum polyblepharum*

10 *Pieris japonica* 'Variegata'
11 *Lysimachia nummularia* 'Aurea'
12 *Primula denticulata*
13 *Dicentra formosa*
14 *Lamium maculatum* 'Beacon Silver'
15 *Berberis thunbergii* f. *atropurpurea*
16 *Luzula sylvatica* 'Marginata'
17 *Heucherella tiarelloides*

18 *Aucuba japonica* 'Picturata'
19 *Polygonatum* x *hybridum*
20 *Clematis alpina* 'Columbine'
21 *Ligularia dentata* 'Othello'
22 *Astilbe* 'Aphrodite'
23 *Hosta* 'Wide Brim'
24 *Melissa officinalis* 'Aurea'
25 *Geum rivale* 'Album'
26 *Hydrangea quercifolia* 'Snow Flake'

'Aureum', with its mound of soft gold leaves that tend to scorch if the plant is grown in hot, direct sunlight.

Many spring-flowering perennials are particularly fond of cool shady positions. The lilac, carmine and rose drumstick flowerheads of *Primula denticulata*, the elegant, arching stems and delicate, pendulous white flowers of *Polygonatum* x *hybridum* (Solomon's seal) and the pink hearts of *Dicentra formosa* (bleeding heart), nestling above the finely cut foliage, do best in such conditions. There is plenty of colour during the summer, too, with the striking orange heads of *Ligularia dentata* 'Othello', the feathery, deep pink upright plumes of *Astilbe* 'Aphrodite' and the large white panicles of *Hydrangea quercifolia* 'Snowflake' set against its deeply cut, bold leaves.

Though often found in the margins of ponds, *Primula denticulata* will grow well in any good soil where it is not too sunny or dry.

Coping with Shade

In gardening the word 'shade' can be applied to several areas. The most obvious, and often the most difficult to deal with, is the shade cast directly beneath the crown of a large tree. Although a certain amount of light may filter through the foliage and some direct sunlight may penetrate sideways under the edge of the crown, the light levels generally are low and you will need to select plants that will tolerate not only this but also the relative dryness and competition caused by the tree itself, which takes moisture and nutrients from the soil.

Another type of shade, which is actually shadow, is caused by a solid object, such as a wall or fence, intercepting direct sunlight. Planting against such a structure will receive more indirect overhead light than it would under a tree, and in the height of summer it may even receive some direct sunlight in the early morning and late evening.

For this situation you can choose from a wide range of plants that will tolerate light or partial shade. However, the ground conditions here are still likely to be dry because of the 'rain shadow' caused by the structure.

The genus *Geranium* includes an enormous number of perennials, which are almost indispensable in the garden. They are among the most reliable, easy-going plants, requiring very little or no maintenance, and they are generally little affected by pests and diseases. They range in size from tiny, prostrate forms, such as *G.* x *lindavicum* 'Apple Blossom', with its delicately veined, pale pink flowers, to bold, robust forms, such as *G. psilostemon* (**pictured above**), which grows to 90cm (36in) high and has brilliantly intense magenta flowers for many weeks. Some species are suitable for mixed and herbaceous borders, and others for raised beds and rock gardens; yet others make excellent groundcover, particularly the leafy forms, such as *G. ibericum*, with its brilliant dark blue flowers over large dense mounds of dark foliage, and *G. renardii*, which is smaller and has neat grey-green leaves and pale violet flowers.

As long as they are not exposed to extremes of drought or moisture, geraniums will thrive in almost any soil and, depending on the species or cultivar, almost any position. The alpine types need full sun, while others, such as *G. oxonianum* 'Wargrave Pink', will tolerate light shade. The tall *G. phaeum* and low, spreading, *G. macrorrhizum* can even be grown in a woodland situation or as underplantings to deciduous shrubs.

Patio
Gardens

One of the most important areas of a garden, from both a visual and a practical point of view, is the link between the house and garden itself. This is the point at which garden activities spill into the house, and vice versa. For practical reasons the patio area needs to be of a hard, level material, such as stone, brick or gravel, laid on a bed of hardcore to provide all-weather access and a space on which to relax when the conditions are suitable. Ideally, it should be positioned near to access into the house and preferably be in a position that is sunny for at least part of each day.

Simple square or rectangular patios are fine from a functional point of view, but they can be rather uninteresting. The design shown overleaf extends the square patio slightly to accommodate a small change in level by creating upper- and lower-level squares, linked at the corner. Joining the two is a raised pool, which makes an attractive focal point both from the patio itself and also seen from the house.

Balancing the pool on the other side is a simple pergola, planted with a mixture of climbing plants, which provide a degree of shelter and separation from the rest of the garden. Around the paved areas planting is generous to help create a comfortable feeling of enclosure, with many of the lower, edging plants spilling over to soften the rather stiff, geometric lines of the paved areas. Equally important in this arrangement is the link between the patio and lawn so that there is space to extend further out into the garden on special occasions.

• option 1

Gravel Patio Garden

Using gravel instead of a more traditional, rigid surfacing material such as stone flags or brick is not only an economic solution but also a great way to display the plants around it, because you can spread the gravel underneath and between them both to act as a weed-suppressing mulch and to enhance the characteristics of foliage and flower.

Many plants respond well to this treatment, which keeps root systems cool and moist, even when the above-ground stems and leaves are in full sun. The planting scheme for this patio garden is particularly exciting, because not only does it have pockets of interest all year round but it also includes many types of plant that are valuable to insects and birds. There is plenty of structure – from the evergreen *Pyracantha*

'Orange Glow', with its clusters of white, pungent flowers in spring and masses of orange autumn berries, to *Buddleja* 'Lochinch', which has a mass of silver-grey foliage and pale blue flower spikes (which are adored by butterflies) and the beautiful shrub rose, *Rosa* 'Geranium', which has pink flowers and huge scarlet-orange hips in autumn. Perennials in this design range from the architectural *Hosta plantaginea* and its scented spikes of summer flowers to the finely cut leaves and persistent yellow daisies of *Coreopsis verticillata* 'Grandiflora'.

There is plenty of interest, even in the depths of winter, with the bright gold, low mound of *Juniperus × pfitzeriana* 'Gold Coast' and the scarlet berry clusters on the evergreen shrub *Skimmia japonica* 'Veitchii', which is situated near to the house so that it can be fully appreciated even in poor weather.

other ideas

GRAVEL GARDEN IN SHADE

The planting scheme for the patio gravel garden uses plants that are happy in full sun for most of the day. If the area is in shade or if there is direct sun for only part of the day, you would need to substitute species that need less sun. For example, the sun-loving buddleja could be replaced by the pale blue *Hydrangea aspera* subsp. *sargentiana*, and the lavender could be changed for *Liriope muscari* (lilyturf) or the taller *Geranium phaeum*. An alternative to the jasmine for a shady position is the honeysuckle *Lonicera periclymenum* 'Graham Thomas' (**pictured above**), and the evergreen crimson-flowered *Berberidopsis corallina* (coral plant) could be used instead of *Rosa* 'Zéphirine Drouhin'. For berry interest replace *Rosa* 'Geranium' with *Viburnum opulus* 'Compactum', and use *Rhododendron luteum* as a scented substitute for the philadelphus. The aromatic fennel will not do well in shade, so use *Choisya ternata* (Mexican orange blossom) or the red-flowered *Ribes viburnifolium* and replace *Paeonia lactiflora* 'Sarah Bernhardt' with the dwarf, long-flowering *Hydrangea macrophylla* 'Forever Pink'.

The golden foliage of the meadowsweet, *Filipendula ulmaria* 'Aurea', will make a bright splash in place of the coreopsis. *Hyacinthoides non-scripta* (bluebell) is a useful, strappy-leaved alternative to the scented purple-flowered iris. *Taxus baccata* 'Repens Aurea' is a low-growing golden foliage substitute for the juniper, and *Anemone hupehensis* var. *japonica* 'Bressingham Glow' equals the dwarf aster in flower interest.

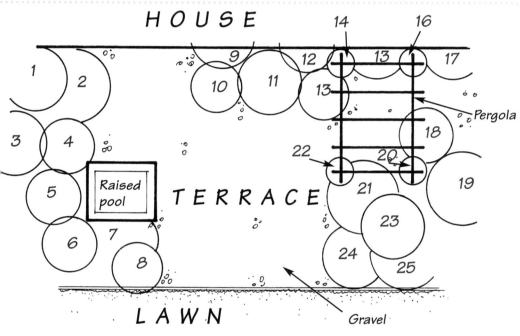

planting key

1 *Pyracantha* 'Orange Glow'
2 *Erica darleyensis* 'Silberschmelze'
3 *Buddleja* 'Lochinch'
4 *Skimmia japonica* 'Rubella'
5 *Foeniculum vulgare* 'Giant Bronze'
6 *Paeonia lactiflora* 'Sarah Bernhardt'
7 *Coreopsis verticillata* 'Grandiflora'
8 *Iris graminea*
9 *Cotoneaster atropurpureus* 'Variegatus'
10 *Skimmia japonica* 'Veitchii'
11 *Mahonia aquifolium* 'Apollo'
12 *Euonymus fortunei* 'Emerald 'n' Gold'
13 *Geranium phaeum* 'Album'
14 *Jasminum officinale*
15 *Sarcococca confusa*
16 *Hedera helix* 'Tricolor'
17 *Lavandula × intermedia* 'Twickel Purple'
18 *Persicaria affinis* 'Superba'
19 *Rosa* 'Geranium'
20 *Lonicera periclymenum* 'Graham Thomas'
21 *Hosta plantaginea*
22 *Rosa* 'Zéphirine Drouhin'
23 *Philadelphus* 'Silberregen'
24 *Juniperus × pfitzeriana* 'Gold Coast'
25 *Aster novi-belgii* 'Jenny'

● option 2
Colour-themed Patio Garden

When you are planning a small garden, or even a bed with a specific colour theme in mind, it is usually not enough simply to put together a collection of plants with the appropriately coloured flowers or foliage. It is also important to provide a number of linking plants with neutral or complementary colours to act as buffers and foils.

In this garden the principal colours of blue and yellow are made more effective by some white-flowered plants, such as *Rosa* 'Climbing Iceberg' and a scented evergreen shrub *Carpenteria californica*, which is set against the brilliant blue flower masses of the larger *Ceanothus* 'Concha'. The lemon-yellow flowers of the daylily *Hemerocallis* 'Hyperion' and the deeper gold of *Rosa* 'Golden Showers', trained up the pergola post, are

complemented by golden-yellow foliage – the small evergreen *Ilex crenata* 'Golden Gem' and the toothed leaves of *Physocarpus opulifolius* 'Dart's Gold'.

Shape and form are also important here. The tall *Agapanthus* 'Blue Giant', with its strappy leaves and large blue globular flowerheads, is next to the neat, bushy *Aster novi-belgii* 'Schneekissen', with its late-summer, tiny, white daisies. The bold leaves of *Rodgersia pinnata*

'Superba' are set against the tiny, glossy evergreen leaves and blue flowers of low-growing *Ceanothus thyrsiflorus* var. *repens*.

Although mostly a spring and summer garden, there is plenty to avoid winter drabness. The evergreens, the winter-flowering *Erica carnea* 'Springwood White' and the dead but attractive stems and flowerheads of *Miscanthus sinensis* 'Strictus' and the agapanthus continue to provide structure and interest into winter.

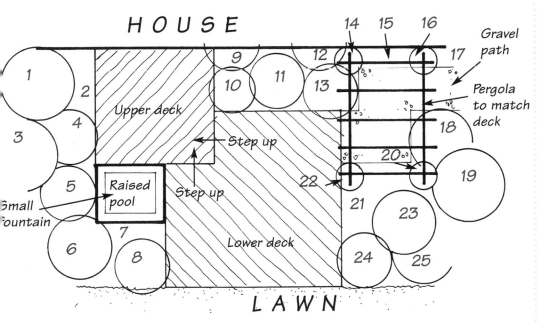

PATIO GARDEN WITH STRONG COLOURS

The white, blue and yellow colour theme of the patio planting is deliberately designed to be restful. However, you could enliven it and make it more energetic by creating a series of hot spots. One excellent plant for this purpose is the brilliant red *Crocosmia* 'Emberglow', which could replace the pale lemon hemerocallis. The delicate grey foliage and blue flowers of the caryopteris might be replaced by the frilly, brilliant orange flowers of *Papaver orientale* 'Curlilocks', while the deep red *Penstemon* 'Andenken an Friedrich Hahn' would be a good alternative to the upright miscanthus, and a dwarf scarlet *Rhododendron* from the Gertrud Schäle Group could replace the *Ceanothus thyrsiflorus* var. *repens*.

You could create an even richer, warmer feel by introducing some purples and deep yellows. *Berberis ottawensis* 'Superba', which has orange-red tones in autumn, would be a good replacement for the sorbus, while the golden-leaved, evergreen *Choisya ternata* 'Sundance' could be grown against the house wall instead of *Ceanothus* 'Concha'. The aster could be replaced by *Lysimachia ciliata* 'Firecracker', which has dark chocolate-purple leaves and golden flowers, and the deep gold, brown-centred flowers of *Rudbeckia fulgida* var. *deamii* (**pictured above**) would be a good alternative to the santolina (cotton lavender). Finally, replace the white *Clematis florida* 'Sieboldii' with the rich purple, velvety flowers of *C.* 'Royal Velours'.

planting key

1 *Ceanothus* 'Concha'
2 *Erica carnea* 'Springwood White'
3 *Carpenteria californica*
4 *Ilex crenata* 'Golden Gem'
5 *Miscanthus sinensis* 'Strictus'
6 *Agapanthus* 'Blue Giant'
7 *Aster novi-belgii* 'Schneekissen'
8 *Hemerocallis* 'Hyperion'
9 *Jasminum nudiflorum*
10 *Caryopteris clandonensis* 'Kew Blue'
11 *Spiraea nipponica* 'Snowmound'
12 *Hedera helix* 'Oro di Bogliasco'
13 *Geranium ibericum*
14 *Rosa* 'Climbing Iceberg'
15 *Hosta* 'Royal Standard'
16 *Clematis alpina*
17 *Santolina chamaecyparissus*
18 *Liriope muscari*
19 *Sorbus koehneana*
20 *Rosa* 'Golden Showers'
21 *Rodgersia pinnata* 'Superba'
22 *Clematis florida* 'Sieboldii'
23 *Physocarpus opulifolius* 'Dart's Gold'
24 *Ceanothus thyrsiflorus* var. *repens*
25 *Oenothera macrocarpa*

• **option 3**

Patio with Year-round Interest

Because of their proximity to the house, terraces and patios are important even in winter when they are not in use but can be viewed from indoors.

A good design will provide plenty of attractive plants to create focal points, particularly flowers, for as long as possible, and this design includes the evergreen climber *Clematis cirrhosa* var. *balearica*, whose scented, greenish-cream flowers appear in late winter, as well as those that will bloom until late autumn and beyond, such as the brilliant, pinky-red stars of *Schizostylis coccinea* 'Major' and the long-flowering evergreen shrub *Viburnum tinus* 'Eve Price', which bears clusters of pink-tinged white flowers through winter.

There is much variety in the flowers themselves, from the silver-blue, thistle-like heads of *Eryngium bourgatii*

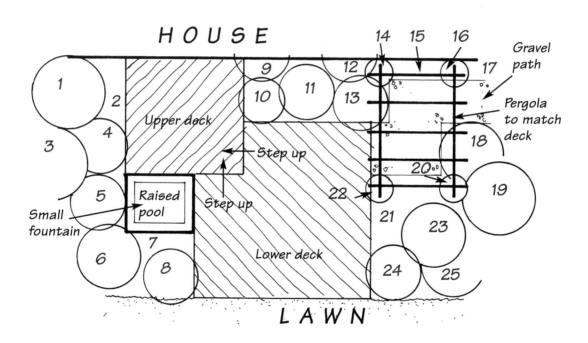

1 *Viburnum tinus* 'Eve Price'
2 *Eryngium bourgatii*
3 *Weigela florida* 'Florida Variegata'
4 *Berberis thunbergii* 'Dart's Red Lady'
5 *Stipa calamagrostis*
6 *Agapanthus campanulatus* var. *albidus*
7 *Solidago* 'Crown of Rays'
8 *Schizostylis coccinea* 'Major'

9 *Euonymus fortunei* 'Silver Queen'
10 *Leucanthemum superbum* 'Aglaia'
11 *Spiraea japonica* 'Goldflame'
12 *Hydrangea anomala* subsp. *petiolaris*
13 *Astilbe arendsii* 'Irrlicht'
14 *Jasminum officinale* 'Argenteovariegatum'
15 *Tellima grandiflora* Rubra Group

16 *Clematis cirrhosa* var. *balearica*
17 *Perovskia* 'Blue Spire'
18 *Helleborus argutifolius*
19 *Elaeagnus pungens* 'Gilt Edge'
20 *Rosa* 'Schoolgirl'
21 *Polygonatum multiflorum*
22 *Clematis* 'Ville de Lyon'
23 *Cornus alba* 'Aurea'
24 *Hypericum moserianum* 'Tricolor'
25 *Dianthus* 'Doris'

(sea holly), to the large, white, globular clusters of *Agapanthus campanulatus* var. *albidus* and the classic, double, coppery-yellow heads of the climbing rose *Rosa* 'Schoolgirl' on the pergola.

Scent is an extra dimension. The sweet smell of the white trumpets of *Jasminum officinale* 'Argenteovariegatum' is almost

lost among the silver-variegated foliage, while the aromatic pungency of the upright blue flower spikes and grey leaves of *Perovskia* 'Blue Spire' (Russian sage) are evident in late summer. The classic 'clove' scent of *Dianthus* 'Doris' along the sunny edge of the bed also provides pleasure in early summer.

White flower interest is complemented by the range of foliage colours and textures, and it is worth noting that almost all the plants in this scheme provide excellent material for bringing indoors either as individual cut flowers or for artistic mixed arrangements.

The long-lasting elegant flower spikes of *Stipa calamagrostis* make an excellent foil to the larger leaved shrubs and perennials.

plant group

CORNUS (DOGWOODS)

The genus *Cornus* includes deciduous trees and shrubs and a few woody perennials, all outstanding in flower, foliage, stem and even berries, and it is usually possible to grow at least one form of this versatile plant. In size they vary from the tiny, suckering *C. canadensis* (dwarf cornel) (**pictured above**), at about 20cm (8in) high, which forms carpets of white, star-shaped flowers in a shady position, to the tree-like *C. kousa*, which has the brilliant autumn colour that is a feature of the genus. These flowering dogwoods are striking plants, but they do best in a sheltered, lightly shaded site, and in soil that is humus-rich and moisture-retentive, and ideally neutral or slightly acid.

Species such as *C. sanguinea* (common dogwood), *C. alba* (red-barked dogwood) and *C. mas* (cornelian cherry) are perfectly hardy. The flowers on these are less flamboyant, but not unattractive, especially as they are often followed by black-blue, violet or white fruits. *C. mas* bears fluffy yellow flowers on bare stems early in the year, making it an excellent winter plant. Forms of *C. alba* and *C. sanguinea* are noted not only for their interesting foliage – gold, variegated, purple-tinged – but also for their winter stems, which can range from bright green to straw yellow, orange and near black. This latter group is tolerant of a wide range of soils and situations, but full sun is needed for good foliage and stem colour. Dogwoods grown for these qualities should be pruned hard back at the end of every winter or at least biennially.

Pruning Flowering Shrubs

Most flowering shrubs benefit from regular annual pruning to remove old flowerheads and wood and to encourage new shoots and large, healthy flowers. One of the commonest gardening complaints is that a particular shrub has not flowered again, but the reason is almost certain to be that premature pruning has removed all the flower buds. With some exceptions, shrubs fall into two main categories: those that flower on stems formed in the previous growing season, and those that flower on stems produced in the current season. The former tend to be those plants that flower between early winter and late spring; plants in the latter group usually flower from the beginning or middle of summer right through to late autumn.

Shrubs that flower in the first half of the year on the previous year's wood should be pruned immediately after they have flowered. This group includes popular plants such as

mahonias, *Viburnum bodnantense* and *V. tinus* (laurustinus), forsythia, *Hamamelis* species (witch hazel), camellias, evergreen ceanothus (**pictured right**), weigela, and mophead and

lacecap hydrangeas. Those shrubs that flower in the latter half of the year on new shoots should be pruned in late winter to early spring, just before they begin to make new growth. Plants in this category include buddleja, caryopteris, deciduous ceanothus, ceratostigma and cultivars of *Hydrangea paniculata*.

Courtyard Gardens

A modern courtyard is usually created when an outdoor space is enclosed on all sides by solid structures, such as buildings and high walls. Such a garden can provide a wonderful opportunity to create a private space – large or small – in the middle of a town or city, and, because of the high boundaries, you will find a tremendous variation in conditions in even the smallest garden, ranging from cool, moist shade to hot, dry sun, which can extend the planting possibilities enormously. In addition, the physical arrangement of such a garden means that it can be relatively sheltered not only from prevailing winds but also from the noise and bustle of the outside world.

By their nature many courtyard gardens are square or rectangular, such as the modest garden shown in the design overleaf. Rather than do the obvious and build a square patio in the centre of the garden with a narrow perimeter border, this design has turned it through 45 degrees to create a completely different look. This arrangement makes the planting beds comparatively deep, and there is more effective space to plant larger shrubs without the area becoming claustrophobic.

The main paving is of natural, randomly placed, rectangular stone to match the courtyard walls. By contrast, however, old bricks are used in front of the house door and the gateway into the street behind, and this brick is also used to edge the stone paving and to link these areas.

• option 1

Cottage-garden-style Courtyard

The dominant features of most, if not all, courtyards are the walls or other structures surrounding them. These are a great asset: they not only allow the growth of climbers or wall shrubs, offering extra height and depth of planting, but they also create areas of sun and shade, providing a range of growing conditions.

This design for a cottage-garden effect uses shrubs and climbers to give a structure and framework for smaller perennials and other plants. The evergreen, blue-flowered *Ceanothus dentatus* is trained against the sunny wall, where it will thrive, while the blue and mauve *Clematis* 'Barbara Jackman' and the red-flowered honeysuckle *Lonicera americana* will do better on the adjacent wall which receives only morning sun.

Shrubby structure is provided by the long-flowering white *Rosa rugosa* 'Alba', which has large orange hips, *Hydrangea aspera* subsp. *sargentiana*, which has green-grey leaves and large, flat heads of pale mauvy-blue flowers and does best in the cool shade, and the purple-leaved *Berberis* x *ottawensis* 'Superba', which develops its best colour in full sun, when the outstanding orange-red autumn colour can also be seen to advantage.

Traditional cottage-garden perennials provide a range of texture and colour. These include the tall, felty spikes and lemon yellow saucers of *Verbascum* 'Gainsborough', the lovely rich purple bells and soft foliage mounds of *Aquilegia vulgaris* var. *stellata* 'Ruby Port', at home in sun or shade, and the excellent low groundcover plant, *Bergenia cordifolia* 'Purpurea', which has glossy foliage, red-tinged in winter, and purple flowers.

other ideas

COLOUR-THEMED COTTAGE-GARDEN COURTYARD

The planting for the cottage-garden version of the courtyard scheme includes a range of flower and foliage colour that more or less covers the spectrum. However, the mood of the garden could be changed by replacing a few plants and altering the colour emphasis. You could omit strong red and orange flowers, which tend to stand out, replacing them with softer, quieter colours to give a calmer feel. For example, the potentilla, poppy and camellia could be replaced with a yellow *Potentilla recta* 'Warrenii', *Lonicera periclymenum* 'Graham Thomas', which has creamy-yellow flowers, the fragrant, cerise pink *Rosa* 'Zéphirine Drouhin', the single, pink *Papaver orientale* 'Mrs Perry' (**pictured above**) and the single, white *Camellia japonica* 'Alba Simplex'.

Alternatively, you might want to make the garden altogether more lively and vibrant, in which case you would need to introduce more bright, possibly 'hot' colours, especially reds and oranges. To increase the number of red flowers, replace the dianthus, monarda and salvia with the salmon-red *Dianthus* 'Diane', the bright red *Monarda* 'Cambridge Scarlet' and the purple-leaved, red-flowered *Lobelia* 'Queen Victoria'. To increase the amount of orange in the garden you could change the jasmine, phlox and scabious with the orange-scarlet trumpets of *Campsis* x *tagliabuana* 'Madame Galen', the upright spikes of *Phlox paniculata* 'Prince of Orange' and the intense orange of the long-flowering *Geum* 'Borisii'.

Courtyard wall

Gate

Brick edging

Random rectangular Yorkstone paving

HOUSE

Brick paving

HOUSE

planting key

1 *Ceanothus dentatus*
2 *Iris* 'Butterscotch Kiss'
3 *Potentilla* 'Gibson's Scarlet'
4 *Rosa rugosa* 'Alba'
5 *Verbascum* 'Gainsborough'
6 *Clematis* 'Barbara Jackman'
7 *Dianthus* 'Devon Glow'
8 *Astilbe* x *arendsii* 'Hyazinth'
9 *Monarda* 'Snow Queen'
10 *Hydrangea aspera* subsp. *sargentiana*
11 *Lonicera americana*
12 *Aquilegia vulgaris* var. *stellata* 'Ruby Port'
13 *Phlox carolina* 'Bill Baker'
14 *Salvia nemorosa* 'Lubecca'
15 *Schizophragma hydrangeoides*
16 *Camellia japonica* 'Adolphe Audusson'
17 *Rosa* 'Paul's Scarlet Climber'
18 *Echinacea purpurea* 'White Swan'
19 *Scabiosa caucasica* 'Clive Greaves'
20 *Jasminum officinale* f. *affine*
21 *Papaver orientale* 'Marcus Perry'
22 *Bergenia cordifolia* 'Purpurea'
23 *Delphinium* Blue Bird Group
24 *Berberis* x *ottawensis* 'Superba'
25 *Lavandula angustifolia*

• option 2

Shady Courtyard Garden

There may be occasions when the enclosing walls around a courtyard effectively prevent any direct sunlight from reaching the ground within it. Many plants will, however, grow perfectly happily in these restricted conditions because there will still be reasonable amounts of natural daylight from directly overhead.

On the walls the fragrant creamy-yellow flowers of *Lonicera periclymenum* (common honeysuckle, woodbine) and the raspberry-pink stars of *Clematis* 'Lincoln Star' provide highlights, as does the variegated ivy *Hedera helix* 'Tricolor'. Bright spots of colour are excellent in darkish areas, and the scheme includes *Choisya ternata* 'Sundance', with pale gold-coloured, evergreen leaves and scented white flowers in late spring, the deciduous

azalea *Rhododendron* 'Gibraltar', which has large orange-pink trumpets, and *Caltha palustris* var. *alba*, a form of marsh marigold with white flowers. Variations in foliage form and colour add an extra dimension. The narrow glossy spikes of *Iris foetidissima* (stinking gladwyn) contrast with the bold heart-shaped, green-edged gold leaves of *Hosta* 'Gold Standard' and the rough-edged, leaves of *Rubus henryi* var. *bambusarum*.

The period of interest is long, starting with the tiny yellow flowers of *Jasminum nudiflorum* (winter jasmine) and lasting until the late-summer flowers of *Anemone hupehensis* 'Hadspen Abundance', with its large pink, yellow-centred saucers, and *Aconitum* 'Bressingham Spire'. In winter any evergreens are enhanced by the white berries of *Symphoricarpos doorenbosii* 'White Hedge' and the tiny red fruits on creeping *Cornus canadensis* (dwarf cornel).

plant group

FERNS

Hardy ferns are sometimes neglected, probably because they do not have dramatic, brightly coloured flowers or startling foliage. Individually, however, they are handsome, refined plants with green foliage of many shades – sometimes with hints of gold, copper and silver. Most ferns prefer a cool, shady position, either sheltered by the light overhead foliage of deciduous trees and shrubs or in a sunless position.

Ferns should be allowed to develop their natural habit, whether it is the arching mound of *Matteuccia struthiopteris* (shuttlecock or ostrich fern, **pictured above**), which early in the year looks like a bright green shuttlecock, or the neat hummocks of *Adiantum pedatum* (maidenhair fern), with its tiny leaflets along slender black stalks. Some ferns, such as *Polystichum polyblepharum* (Japanese tassel fern), are evergreen and make excellent groundcover. Others, like enormous *Osmunda regalis* (flowering or royal fern), are deciduous and look particularly striking as they unfurl their fresh green fronds in late spring.

Athyrium niponicum var. *pictum* (Japanese painted fern), with its delicate silver-grey leaves, and *Dryopteris erythrosora* (buckler fern), with pinkish-coppery hues, prefer a sheltered spot in moisture-retentive soil, but others are more robust such as *Dryopteris felix-mas* (male fern).

Diagram labels: Courtyard wall, Gate, Brick edging, Random rectangular Yorkstone paving, Brick paving, HOUSE, HOUSE

planting key

1 *Jasminum nudiflorum*
2 *Iris foetidissima*
3 *Heuchera micrantha* var. *diversifolia* 'Bressingham Bronze'
4 *Symphoricarpos doorenbosii* 'White Hedge'
5 *Polygonatum odoratum* var. *pluriflorum* 'Variegatum'
6 *Hedera helix* 'Tricolor'
7 *Aquilegia* 'Crimson Star'
8 *Campanula glomerata* 'Purple Pixie'
9 *Anemone hupehensis* 'Hadspen Abundance'
10 *Choisya ternata* 'Sundance'
11 *Rubus henryi* var. *bambusarum*
12 *Melissa officinalis* 'Aurea'
13 *Hosta* 'Gold Standard'
14 *Caltha palustris* var. *alba*
15 *Lonicera periclymenum*
16 *Hydrangea serrata* 'Grayswood'
17 *Hedera helix* 'Goldchild'
18 *Digitalis lutea*
19 *Iris sibirica* 'Perry's Blue'
20 *Clematis* 'Lincoln Star'
21 *Erythronium* 'Pagoda'
22 *Cornus canadensis*
23 *Aconitum* 'Bressingham Spire'
24 *Rhododendron* 'Gibraltar' (deciduous azalea)
25 *Epimedium rubrum*

• option 3

Minimalist Courtyard Garden

This design adopts a minimalist approach to the planting, which not only creates a greater feeling of space but also allows the various plants to be appreciated as individual features in their own right rather than just as a small part of a more tightly packed, traditional border.

Each plant has been carefully chosen for its distinctive characteristics. These range from the huge, bold leaves

and brilliant autumn colour of the vine *Vitis coignetiae* on the wall to the delicate, hazy, arching grassy mound of *Stipa arundinacea* (pheasant's tail grass). Plants with brightly coloured flowers have been largely avoided in favour of those with more subtle tones, such as the long-lasting frothy, cream-coloured panicles of *Aruncus dioicus* (goatsbeard) with its finely cut foliage, or attractive shapes, such as the handsome purple, green and cream spikes of *Acanthus mollis* (bear's breeches), which rise above dramatic, glossy foliage.

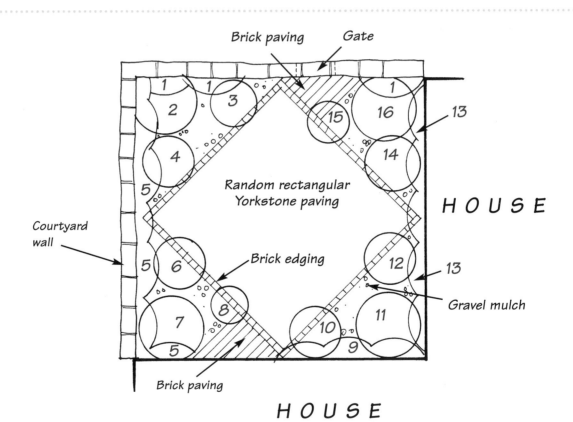

planting key

1 *Lonicera hildebrandiana*
2 *Elaeagnus pungens* 'Maculata'
3 *Rheum* 'Ace of Hearts'
4 *Nandina domestica* 'Richmond'
5 *Vitis coignetiae*
6 *Acanthus mollis*
7 *Corylus maxima* 'Purpurea'
8 *Hosta* 'Big Daddy'
9 *Berberidopsis corallina*
10 *Aruncus dioicus*
11 *Phyllostachys aureosulcata* 'Spectabilis'
12 *Chamaecyparis pisifera* 'Filifera Aurea'
13 *Actinidia kolomikta*
14 *Berberis thunbergii* 'Red Chief'
15 *Stipa arundinacea*
16 *Fatsia japonica*

Evergreens, such as the conifer *Chamaecyparis pisifera* 'Filifera Aurea', with its arching mound of golden, thread-like branchlets, and the striking green- and yellow-stemmed bamboo

Phyllostachys aureosulcata 'Spectabilis' provide a framework of permanent interest, with more seasonal colour coming from the deciduous plants, which include the purple leaves of the shrubby *Berberis thunbergii* 'Red Chief', the large, red-tinged leaves and dramatic flower spikes of *Rheum* 'Ace of Hearts' and the pink, cream and green foliage of the climber *Actinidia kolomikta*. *Lonicera hildebrandiana* (giant Burmese honeysuckle) grows well in the more sheltered environment of a courtyard, providing masses of dark, evergreen leaves and clusters of creamy-yellow, sweetly scented flowers in summer.

The bold spikes and glossy green leaves of *Acanthus mollis* (bear's breeches) make it an eye-catching addition to any garden.

Minimalist Planting

Apart from the obvious advantage of having fewer plants to look after, minimalist planting is an opportunity to display plants in a more individual yet restrained way. With lots of space around it, a plant can develop its natural shape and form with the minimum of interference. Any pruning will be purely for the benefit of the plant and not, for example, due to it blocking a path or encroaching over other plants.

Plants used in this way must be attractive and able to stand alone on their own merits. There are no rules about which plants are suitable for this style of planting, but architectural plants with a distinctive habit, bold leaves or a long flowering period are particularly appropriate. Bamboos and tall grasses, such as *Miscanthus* and *Stipa* (feather grass) species, make elegant focal points, while large shrubs like *Mahonia* and *Aralia* species stand out, because of their dramatic leaves. Some perennials are suitable:

plant them in groups to create a more dramatic effect – acanthus (bear's breeches), hosta, agapanthus and *Hemerocallis* cultivars (daylily) are all excellent, long-lived and relatively trouble-free examples of plants for this style, as are the geraniums *G. phaeum* and *G. ibericum*.

plant focus

BAMBOOS

Until comparatively recently bamboos have not received good garden press, and many people regard them as large, uninteresting and invasive plants. In reality, there are dozens if not hundreds of species, which range in size from less than a metre (3ft) high to jungle giants of 10m (33ft) and more.

They are members of the grass family and without exception have relatively upright stems and grass-like leaves. These characteristics can vary tremendously, however, and as in many woody plants, there are cultivars with different coloured stems – green, black, yellow, striped – and foliage. Many bamboos are perfectly hardy and will grow well in a temperate climate provided that they are sheltered from cold, drying winds and are planted in a reasonably fertile soil that does not become bone-dry.

Their habit of growth falls into two main categories. Some form a clump that slowly increases in diameter year by year, creating a uniform, shapely mass. Some spread by means of underground stolons or rhizomes, which can emerge several metres (yards) from the original plant. In most gardens, clump-forming species are more desirable, and *Fargesia murieliae*, *F. nitida* and *Phyllostachys aurea* (fishpole bamboo, golden bamboo, **pictured above**) make exceptionally fine specimens.

Container Gardening

Containers are an essential part of today's gardens. They bring colour and fragrance to the patio, while choice specimens, not reliably hardy in the wider garden, can be grown close to the shelter of the house. Containers of all shapes and sizes allow gardeners to grow plants requiring specific soil types, and they bring flexibility to the garden in the form of spot colour or temporary focal points.

3

Containers

Containers are an excellent way of growing plants in all sorts of situations, ranging from a tiny balcony garden in the centre of a town to the vast stone terrace of a house in the country. They can be used for seasonal displays, such as spring bulbs and summer bedding, or for more permanent displays of shrubs, perennials and grasses, to give year-round interest. Almost any hollow object that will hold some growing medium, that has drainage holes in the bottom and that will not rot or disintegrate can be used for growing plants, so your choice need not be limited to traditional pots and tubs in terracotta, stone or plastic.

Small containers that can be easily moved can be an advantage if you need to make temporary space on your patio for an alfresco lunch party. The disadvantage of small containers is that they will need watering more frequently in hot, dry and especially windy, weather. Large, dramatic containers are excellent for permanent plantings of shrubs or even small trees, but they must be carefully positioned because, once filled and planted, they may be difficult to move.

If you want to display several containers it is worth arranging them as a composition from the start, in much the same way as you would group together several plants in the ground to create a particular effect. With container plantings you will have the bonus of the colour, texture and shape of the pots or urns, which will make their own contribution to the overall effect.

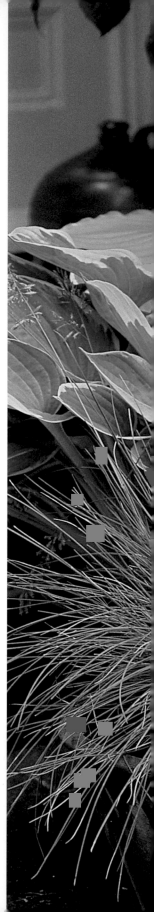

• option 1
Containers for Summer Colour

Growing half-hardy annuals as bedding plants in a variety of containers is an excellent way of providing a bright splash of colour for many weeks throughout the summer. In the arrangement shown here the plants have been selected to create a stunning blue and white effect, which is further enhanced by the choice of pots and planters.

Nemesia caerulea 'Woodcote', which has small, white-centred, blue flowers, makes a gentle, long-flowering mound in a traditionally shaped, blue and white, glazed clay pot. Positioned next to this is a slightly smaller pot in the same style, but with the glazing pattern reversed, and planted with the double, white annual *Dianthus* 'Arctic Star'. Behind these is a more substantial white glazed, round pot with blue motifs, to give some scale

to the grouping. Within this pot, a standard weeping *Fuchsia* 'Annabel' gives height and structure to the whole group, and this is underplanted with the trailing *Petunia* 'Surfinia Blue Vein', with its almost non-stop summer display of white, trumpet-shaped flowers, which have fine purplish-blue veining.

Set off to one side, and providing a distinct contrast to the other, circular containers, is a square, wooden Versailles planter, stained pale blue and planted with a quarter-standard *Argyranthemum frutescens*, with its silvery foliage and white, yellow-centred daisy flowers. Beneath the argyranthemum, a mixture of the blue trailing *Lobelia erinus* 'Sapphire' and the silver-grey leaves of *Helichrysum petiolare* forms a gentle mound that eventually spills over the edge of the planter, softening the rather formal, square lines.

other ideas

COLOUR-THEMED CONTAINERS

For a livelier, more prominent display include reds and oranges, such as the orange-apricot *Diascia* 'Coral Belle', instead of the blue nemesia, and an orange busy lizzie, such as *Impatiens* 'Orange Ice'. The argyranthemum could be replaced by *Abutilon* 'Nabob', with deep red flowers, and underplanted with the scarlet-flowered, ivy-leaved *Pelargonium* 'Narina', a foil for the lime-green *Helichrysum petiolare* 'Limelight'. *Fuchsia* 'Annabel' could be replaced by the red *F.* 'Marinka', trained as a standard and underplanted with the trailing *Verbena* 'Temari Scarlet'.

Yellow and mauve is a striking combination. In the small pots, plant *Astericus* 'Gold Dollar', with yellow daisy-flowers, and a purple-pink busy lizzie, such as *I.* 'Paradise Pascua'. Retain the standard *Argyranthemum frutescens* in the square planter but underplant it with a purple trailing verbena, such as *V.* 'Topaz', mixed with the all-yellow *Bidens ferulifolia* and *Helichrysum petiolare* 'Goring Silver'.

The largest container needs height. The variegated foliage of *Abutilon milleri* is mottled with gold and the orange-yellow flowers have purple centres. Around the edge the dark green and purple *Heliotropium* 'Princess Marina' could be juxtaposed with trailing white lobelia.

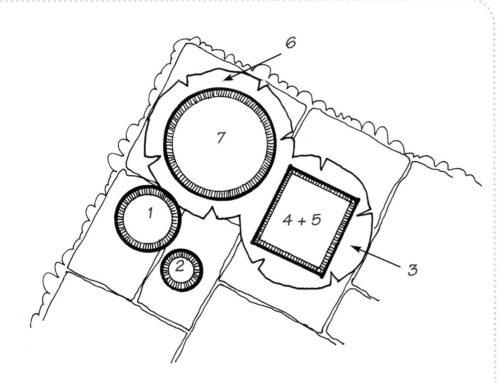

planting key

1 *Nemesia caerulea* 'Woodcote'
2 *Dianthus* 'Arctic Star'
3 *Argyranthemum frutescens* (standard)
4 *Lobelia erinus* 'Sapphire'
5 *Helichrysum petiolare* (silver-grey)
6 *Fuchsia* 'Annabel' (weeping standard)
7 *Petunia* 'Surfina Blue Vein'

• option 2

Year-round Container Planting

Although containers on patios have long been associated with displaying summer bedding plants, which must be replaced annually, there is no reason why more permanent displays cannot be achieved with hardy plants, such as dwarf trees and shrubs, perennials and bulbs.

In permanent plantings it is vital that each plant earns its place in the grouping, and this collection includes just such species, which have been carefully selected to provide colour, form and texture for long periods.

The structure is provided by the coral bark maple, *Acer palmatum* 'Sango-kaku'. It creates a lovely, elegant backdrop of greeny-yellow leaves through summer and

good autumn colour, but most striking are its brilliant coral-red winter stems. Equally valuable is the neatly trimmed mophead *Buxus sempervirens* (common box), which gives a tight, architectural evergreen form throughout the year to contrast with the looser forms of flowers and leaves of the plants around it.

Spring colour comes early with the golden-yellow crocus interplanted with the dense carpeting *Veronica peduncularis*

'Georgia Blue', its blue and white flowers trailing over the sides from late spring to early summer. Flowering for even longer is the perennial pansy, *Viola* 'Clementina', which has large, dark blue flowers. The hardy, gold-leaved *Fuchsia* 'Genii' makes a splash from summer to early autumn, and in late winter the red bark of the maple is a bright backdrop to the long-lasting pink flower spikes of the winter heather *Erica carnea* 'Pink Spangles'.

plant group

COLOURFUL STEMS

There are many plants, particularly shrubs and trees, whose particular appeal lies in the colour of their stems. These may not be fully apparent until autumn and winter, when the plant has shed its leaves, making such plants ideal for the winter garden.

Stem colour can vary through a wide range, from white, yellow and bright green to orange, red, black and coral pink. Forms of *Cornus alba* (dogwood) are especially popular: the stems of *C. alba* 'Sibirica' are brilliant red, *C. alba* 'Kesselringii' nearly black, and *C. sanguinea* 'Midwinter Fire' a striking egg-yolk orange.

Startling white stems are found in some species of *Rubus* (ornamental raspberries), such as *R. thibetanus*. Many types of *Salix* (willow) have attractive winter stems: those of *S. daphnoides* are violet overlaid with a white bloom, and *S. alba* subsp. *vitellina* 'Britzensis' are deep orange, becoming almost red.

Trees with winter stem interest include *Betula* (birch) – *B. utilis* var. *jacquemontii* has brilliant white bark – and some cherries – *Prunus serrula* has shiny mahogany-coloured bark. The older stems of snakebark maples, like *Acer grosseri* var. *hersii* (**pictured above**), have a more subtle effect, with their cream and green stripes.

1 *Fuchsia* 'Genii'
2 *Viola* 'Clementina'
3 *Buxus sempervirens*
4 *Crocus* (large-flowered yellow)

5 *Veronica peduncularis* 'Georgia Blue'
6 *Acer palmatum* 'Sango-kaku'
7 *Erica carnea* 'Pink Spangles'

• **option 3**

Foliage Plants in Containers

Many plants do not rely simply on flowers for their appeal. Instead, they have foliage that is attractive in its own right because of its colour, size, texture or shape. Given the right cultural conditions, most of these foliage plants can be grown in containers, and when a selection is arranged in a carefully chosen group, the effect can be eye-catching.

There is a distinctive theme to the scheme shown here, which emphasizes plants with narrow, spiky foliage and limits the colours mostly to pinks, purples and silver.

Permanent structure is provided by the dark purple foliage of the Japanese maple *Acer palmatum* 'Bloodgood' with the bonus of brilliant autumn colours, the architectural evergreen *Phormium* 'Jester', which is much less vigorous than the more common *Phormium tenax* and has unusual bright green leaves striped with pinkish-red, and the delicate salmon-pink and white, shrimp-like leaves of the 'top-worked' dwarf willow *Salix integra* 'Hakuro-nishiki'.

There is more emphasis on evergreens in this scheme. The almost black, grass-like foliage of the perennial *Ophiopogon planiscapus* 'Nigrescens' (black lilyturf) and

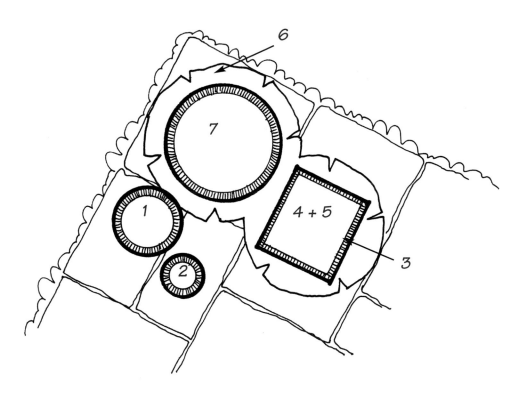

1 *Phormium* 'Jester'
2 *Hedera helix* 'Goldchild'
3 *Salix integra* 'Hakuro-nishiki'
4 *Ophiopogon planiscapus* 'Nigrescens'
5 *Vinca minor* 'Silver Service'
6 *Acer palmatum* 'Bloodgood'
7 *Festuca valesiaca* 'Silbersee'

its spikes of tiny, pinkish flowers followed by black berries combine with the small, gold-splashed leaves and trailing stems of the dwarf ivy *Hedera helix* 'Goldchild' and the neat mounds of slender, silver-blue evergreen leaves of the ornamental grass *Festuca valesiaca* 'Silbersee'. The silver theme is continued with the periwinkle *Vinca minor* 'Silver Service', which has silver-edged, pointed leaves and pale blue flowers and which softens the edge of the Versailles planter.

The dark, dramatic foliage of *Ophiopogon planiscapus* 'Nigrescens' draws the eye and is worth including to add variety to a collection of foliage plants.

Fragrant plants add an extra quality over and above the beauty of flowers, leaves and stems. Scent can be found in all types of plants, from the aromatic foliage of tiny creeping perennials, such as *Thymus serpyllum*, to large flowering trees, such as *Tilia* (lime).

Traditional scented climbers, such as *Lonicera* species (honeysuckle), *Jasminum* species (jasmine) and roses, are ideal for planting over pergolas and arbours. Larger shrubs, including mahonias, viburnums and philadelphus, are more effective if planted in relatively warm, sheltered positions, where their scent lingers. Winter scent, like winter flower, is especially desirable. *Chimonanthus praecox* (wintersweet) produces sweetly scented, yellow-purple flowers in later winter: it is ideal for planting against a sunny wall near the door. This is also a good place for the evergreen *Azara microphylla*, which bears vanilla-scented blooms in early spring.

If space is limited, choose species to provide a succession of scent: the evergreen osmanthus in early spring, *Jasminum officinale* (**pictured above**) in summer and the bulbous *Crinum powellii* in autumn at the front of a sunny border. You can grow scented plants in containers, especially bulbs, such as *Lilium regale* (regal lily), and perennials, like *Hosta* 'Honeybells'.

Siting Containers

Where and how you place containers is probably as important as what you actually put in them. Before you site any containers in the garden, you will need to bear two points in mind. First, consider where they will be seen from and against what type of background; second, choose positions that will provide conditions to suit the types of plant that are growing in the containers.

If they are used as focal points, containers will be viewed from garden seats and sitting areas or from windows in the main rooms of your house. They may be framed between trees or evergreen shrubs or seen through arches. As with feature plants, what is behind a container can affect its appearance: brightly coloured plants and pale containers will be set off to their best advantage in front of a dark surface, such as a yew hedge or dark grey stone wall, but darker containers and plants are better against a light background of silver or gold.

The direction in which the sunlight falls will also affect the appearance of the container. When the sun comes from behind a planted container, it will tend to throw it into shadow from the viewer's side, reducing its visual impact, but sunlight coming from behind and slightly to one side of the viewing point will highlight the front of the planter, picking it out and giving it due prominence.

Windowboxes and Wall Baskets

Windowboxes, hanging baskets and wall baskets are little different from other types of containers. However, most traditional planted containers sit on the ground, while windowboxes and hanging baskets are the perfect solution for those situations where there is no ground space available. That is not to say, of course, that you cannot use them where you do have more space, because they are an excellent way of creating splashes of colour and hot spots where it might be difficult or impossible to create the same effect with more conventional planters.

W ith larger windowboxes it is possible to create plantings to provide some interest almost all year round. Dwarf evergreen shrubs, miniature conifers and winter- or summer-flowering heathers are particularly valuable framework plants for this kind of effect.

Traditional annual bedding plants make it possible to create a wide range of effects, ranging from incredibly busy, multicoloured plantings to restrained, cool colour themes of perhaps just blues and white, or vibrant, hot splashes of red and orange.

Because they are so manageable, plantings in baskets and windowboxes can be changed periodically to reflect the seasons – evergreens for late autumn and winter, dwarf bulbs, such as *Galanthus* species (snowdrop) and crocuses and alpines for spring, and annual bedding for summer and autumn. In particular, windowboxes are a splendid way to grow a small selection of herbs, which can be picked spontaneously to give that straight-from-the-garden taste.

• option 1

Planting for Spring

After a long, cold winter, there is nothing better than to watch spring in the garden, especially if the scene unfolds directly outside your window.

Providing height, yet perfectly in scale with this windowbox 'garden', are the miniature conifer *Juniperus communis* 'Compressa', with its silver-green flame-shape, the neat, bright yellow-green foliage of *Calluna* *vulgaris* 'Ruth Sparkes', which has double white flowers in late summer and, in contrast to these, the tight, purple bun of deciduous *Berberis thunbergii* 'Bagatelle', with its cream and yellow flowers in late spring set against the fresh new leaves.

Alpines come into their own in spring and provide a carpet of colour between the comparatively tall shrubs and the conifer. The cheerful, long-lasting daisies and

fern-like foliage of *Anacyclus pyrethrum* var. *depressus*, the charming pink flowers of *Dianthus* 'Pike's Pink', and the tiny blue bells of *Campanula carpatica* 'Blue Moonlight' contrast perfectly with the golden-edged rosettes of *Arabis ferdinandi-coburgi* 'Old Gold'.

The creeping grey-green mats of *Thymus doefleri* 'Bressingham' trail over the sides. The thyme is covered in minute pink flowers in late spring, and these contrast with the more upright foliage and violet-tinged, white flowers of the miniature pansy *Viola* 'Rebecca'. In the opposite corner, the simple white bells and neat green hummocks of *Campanula carpatica* f. *alba* 'Bressingham White' sit nicely alongside the long-flowering alpine version of the garden scabious, *Cephalaria alpina*, with its tiny, delicate mauve-blue flowerheads nestling above low mounds of evergreen foliage.

plant group

CAMPANULAS

There are campanulas (bellflowers) to suit almost any situation in any size of garden. The main distinguishing feature of the genus is the flower, which is in the form of a bell, hence the common name. Although they are mostly in shades of blue, verging on mauve, there are also white- and pink-flowered forms, such as *C. portenschlagiana* 'Resholdt's Variety' (**pictured above**).

Campanulas are perennials, varying in size from the neat little alpine hummocks of *C. carpatica* at 15–20cm (6–8in) high to the upright stems and milky-pink flowers of *C. lactiflora* 'Loddon Anna' at 1.8m (6ft).

Most campanulas are long-lived and trouble-free, and they are tolerant of a wide range of well-drained soils. The lower, more spreading forms are ideal for the front of borders and for rock or scree gardens, while the taller ones are best used in association with shrubs or as part of a herbaceous border.

The flowering period begins with the alpine campanulas in early spring, and continues, with species such as *C. latifolia*, through summer, and even, with the later-flowering *C. glomerata* 'Purple Pixie', into early autumn. Those with an extended flowering period, include *C. alliarifolia*, which has white pendulous blooms all through the summer, and the 60cm (24in) high *C. trachelium* 'Bernice', which has double, powder-blue flowers over a similar period.

1 *Juniperus communis* 'Compressa'
2 *Calluna vulgaris* 'Ruth Sparkes'
3 *Berberis thunbergii* 'Bagatelle'
4 *Anacyclus pyrethrum* var. *depressus*
5 *Dianthus* 'Pike's Pink'
6 *Campanula carpatica* 'Blue Moonlight'
7 *Arabis ferdinandi-coburgi* 'Old Gold'
8 *Viola* 'Rebecca'
9 *Thymus doefleri* 'Bressingham'
10 *Campanula carpatica* f. *alba* 'Bressingham White'
11 *Cephalaria alpina*

● option 2

Summer Bedding

Traditionally, windowboxes and hanging baskets are used for creating mass displays of brightly coloured, long-lasting annuals. This example contains a medley of colours to provide summer cheer, with habits ranging from upright to trailing so that the container itself is eventually lost from sight beneath a mass of blooms.

Growing plants in a windowbox makes it possible to use startling colour contrasts that in a larger bed or border might be considered somewhat 'over the top'. The almost wax-like blooms of *Fuchsia* 'Lady in Pink' hang from a bushy plant that gives some height to the arrangement and provides support for the more rambling stems and rich yellow, star-shaped flowers of *Thunbergia alata* (black-eyed Susan). The bold purple

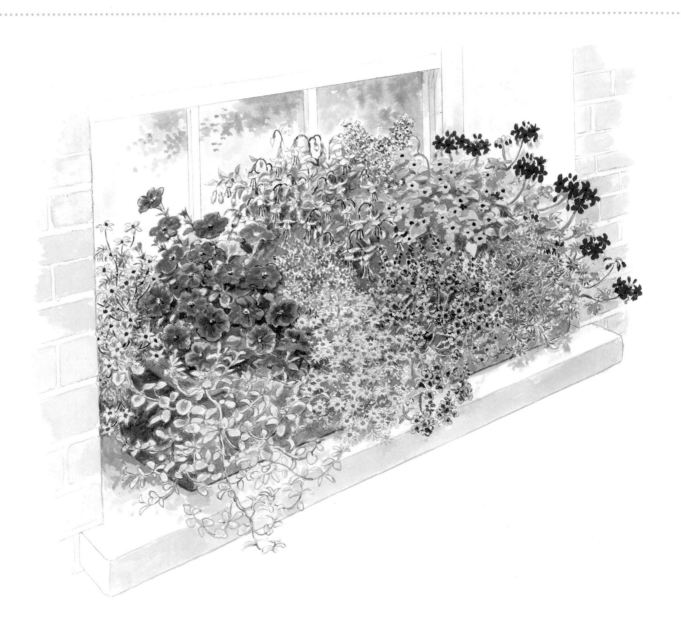

trumpets of the petunia are in marked contrast to both the black-eyed Susan and the finely cut yellow daisies of *Brachyscome* 'Sunburst'. Trailing blue lobelia merges with the equally delicate and abundant tiny white flowers of *Sutera cordata* 'Snowflake'.

Contrasting with the blue and white flowers are the fleshy, ivy-shaped leaves and large, brilliant scarlet flowerheads of a trailing pelargonium, which combines with the smaller gold-centred pale blue flowers of *Felicia amelloides* as they tumble over the sides. In this design, the only concession to pure foliage is the golden version of *Helichrysum petiolare*, with its woolly, rounded leaves and pale, downy-covered trailing stems, which provide a marked contrast to the neat, compact habit and masses of salmon-pink flowerheads covering *Diascia* 'Coral Belle'.

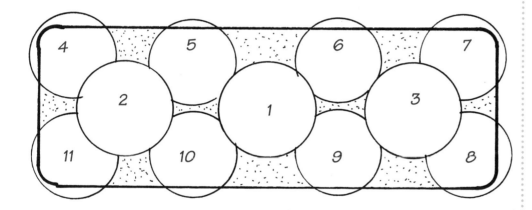

plant group

ANNUALS

Annuals are plants that grow, flower and produce seed in one season. Hardy annuals, such as *Lathyrus odoratus* cultivars (sweet pea), can be sown outdoors early in the year when they wil be undamaged by spring frosts. Others, like forms of *Lobelia erinus*, are half-hardy annuals because they may be damaged by late frosts. They are usually grown in a greenhouse or on a kitchen windowsill until all danger of frost is past, when they can be planted outside.

Annuals are ideal for creating spots of bright colour in a short space of time, although they do need to be replaced each year. Their brief lifecycle means that many ornamental annuals are not only at their peak in summer but also, because they rely solely on seed production to ensure future generations, the flowering itself is usually abundant and over a long period.

Many annuals can be used in beds and borders for informal or formal displays – cultivars of *Salvia*, *Tagetes* (marigold) and *Impatiens* (busy lizzie, **pictured above**) are ideal – but they are also suited for use in containers, from a small pot containing a single, bright red pelargonium, to a mixed hanging basket, a particularly effective way of displaying trailing annuals such as nasturtiums, or a large windowbox or square wooden Versailles planter filled with a wide selection displaying a variety of colour and form. They are also excellent for providing seasonal colour among traditional borders of shrubs and perennials, especially at times when interest might otherwise be lacking.

planting key

1 *Fuchsia* 'Lady in Pink'
2 *Petunia* (purple-flowered)
3 *Thunbergia alata*
4 *Bidens ferulifolia*
5 *Lobelia erinus* 'Sapphire'
6 *Sutera cordata* 'Snowflake'
7 *Pelargonium* (scarlet-flowered, ivy-leaved)
8 *Felicia amelloides*
9 *Diascia* 'Coral Belle'
10 *Brachyscome* 'Sunburst'
11 *Helichrysum petiolare* (golden form)

• option 3

Winter Colour

The beauty of a windowbox planted up for winter is that you do not have to get up from your armchair to appreciate it. Evergreens form the backbone of this particular display, with flowers appearing later on in late winter and early spring.

The low-growing evergreen *Euonymus fortunei* 'Emerald 'n' Gold' provides a brilliant splash of gold and green, and the leaves are attractively tinged with red in cold weather. Winter cold also brings out beautiful tints on the tiny, silver-variegated leaves of *Hedera helix* 'Little

Diamond', which trails over the edges. The variegated leaves are a strong contrast to the huge, rosy-red succulent rosettes of the houseleek *Sempervivum* 'Othello'. This foliage colour is complemented in midwinter by the tiny red bells and deep green leaves of the lime-tolerant heather *Erica carnea* 'December Red'. These flowers last for many weeks, overlapping with the later white spikes of the larger *Erica darleyensis* 'Silberschmelze' and the more spreading crown and soft pink bells of *Erica carnea* 'Springwood Pink'.

Further foliage contrasts come from the small, fleshy, blue-grey rosettes of the alpine *Sedum spathulifolium*

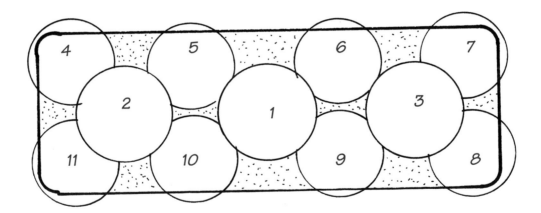

planting key

1 *Euonymus fortunei* 'Emerald 'n' Gold'
2 *Skimmia japonica* 'Rubella'
3 *Erica darleyensis* 'Silberschmelze'

4 *Ajuga reptans* 'Burgundy Glow'
5 *Calluna vulgaris* 'Beoley Gold'
6 *Hedera helix* 'Little Diamond'
7 *Sempervivum* 'Othello'
8 *Erica carnea* 'December Red'

9 *Carex oshimensis* 'Evergold'
10 *Sedum spathulifolium* 'Cape Blanco'
11 *Erica carnea* 'Springwood Pink'

'Cape Blanco' and the glossy pink, cream and purple leaves of the groundcovering bugle *Ajuga reptans* 'Burgundy Glow', and still more colour is provided by the bright golden winter foliage of the summer-flowering heather *Calluna vulgaris* 'Beoley Gold' and the dense clusters of red-budded, white flowers on the dwarf evergreen shrub *Skimmia japonica* 'Rubella'. The narrow arching leaves of the evergreen grass *Carex oshimensis* 'Evergold' are striped yellow, and the habit contrasts well with the neat rosettes of the *Sempervivum* and *Sedum*.

The male flowers of *Skimmia japonica* 'Rubella' are at their best in winter. For berries you will need to plant a female form such as *S. j.* 'Foremanii' nearby.

Heathers (*Erica*, *Calluna* and *Daboecia* species) are among the most useful of dwarf shrubs because of their neat, evergreen habit, long flowering periods and minimal maintenance requirements.

Most make dense, low bushes, from a few centimetres (an inch) to 40–50cm (16–20in) high, and are best displayed in groups of three or more of the same cultivar.

Grow larger heathers like *Erica erigena* and *E. arborea* as single specimens surrounded by smaller heathers or alpines. The famous Scottish heather or ling is *Calluna vulgaris*. There are many coloured forms both in flower – from white through to pink (*c.v.* 'Beoley Gold' is **pictured above**.), mauve and dark purple – and foliage – from pale green and silver through to bright yellow and deep orange-red. With the correct selection, they can be in flower from early summer to late autumn. Most prefer an acid soil; if your soil is alkaline, a good summer-flowering alternative is *Erica vagans* (Cornish heath), which has flowers in white, pink or red. Some cultivars, such as *E. vagans* 'Valerie Proudley', have golden foliage.

The winter heathers *Erica carnea* and *E. darleyensis* also tolerate alkaline soil and produce spikes of bell-shaped flowers in white, pink or red from early winter to late spring.

Choosing a Theme

A theme in a garden in its entirety, or just in a smaller part of it, such as a series of containers or windowboxes, can provide an essential element of unity and create a harmonious effect. Strong themes can be provided by the use of a particular colour, shape or style of hard materials, such as paving, walling and timber. Equally valuable, however, are themes based on planting, particularly where the plants are the most dominant feature.

The most obvious planting theme is one based on colour. It could be a single colour, such as white or blue, although this approach is most effective when it is used as part of a larger garden, subdivided into two or more distinct and individual areas. More common, and probably better suited to a smaller scale, is an approach based on two or more colours. Remember that foliage colour is just as important as flowers in deciding on the theme.

Another approach is to decide on a particular style as a theme – completely informal, as in a cottage garden; severely formal, with limited plant types, perhaps needing regular trimming and with a strong emphasis on symmetry; or a geometric style, with beds, borders and containers based on circles, squares and other bold shapes but using plants with more individual characteristics, such as flowering shrubs, perennials and grasses.

Balconies and Roof Gardens

Almost any outdoor space can be adapted or modified for growing plants, and balconies and flat roofs are no exception. You must first make sure that the structure on which you are going to build your garden is strong enough, and then, if so, provide a suitable growing medium for the plants. The nature of such a garden makes it necessary in all but the largest, strongest structures to keep the plants in some form of container. These can be traditional pots, tubs and urns, which are particularly useful because they can be moved around as and when required, or you can use larger troughs and raised beds, which require less watering and can be filled with more plants for a bolder display.

The small roof garden shown overleaf is fairly typical of many urban houses, and it is just big enough to accommodate a couple of seats. Because they are above ground level, roof and balcony gardens are usually more exposed to prevailing winds, and a trellis screen has been provided on the windward side to create a more sheltered environment. It is combined with a narrow, wooden planting trough along the perimeter, which is the strongest point of a roof garden. To create a balance and give height, there are two large corner containers planted with tall shrubs, and between these is the focal point of a small statue. The floor surface is covered in lightweight wooden decking squares to match the trough and containers.

• option 1

Hot, Dry Roof Garden

Because of their elevated position and increased exposure to the elements, especially prevailing winds, some roof gardens have a hot, dry micro-climate. The plants for such a garden need careful selection to make sure that they are tolerant of these conditions and look good together.

In all gardens, especially small ones, some permanent plant structure is desirable, particularly evergreens. Here, the main fabric is provided by *Elaeagnus pungens* 'Maculata', which has gold-splashed, leathery leaves and is an ideal choice for this situation, and by the golden fastigiate yew *Taxus baccata* 'Standishii', which has a narrow, upright habit and bright year-round foliage.

Further evergreen interest comes from the spiky leaves of *Yucca filamentosa* 'Variegata', which produces spectacular spikes of cream-coloured, bell-shaped flowers, and the variegated form of the gladwyn iris, *Iris foetidissima* 'Variegata', with violet flowers followed in autumn by bright orange seed pods. Silver- and grey-leaved plants are ideal for hot, sunny spots, so the scented *Lavandula* 'Helmsdale' (French lavender) and the small white trumpets of *Convolvulus cneorum* make long-lasting features that will soften the trough edges. Equally eye-catching are the yellow late-spring flowers of the dwarf broom *Cytisus* × *kewensis* and the almost never-ending violet daisies of *Osteospermum ecklonis*.

On the trellis the exotic *Passiflora caerulea* (passionflower) and the long-flowering *Solanum laxum* 'Album' add height and shelter throughout summer.

SCENTED PLANTING FOR A ROOF GARDEN

One of the attractions of a small roof garden or balcony is that as soon as you step on to it you are among the plants, an ideal situation, therefore, to appreciate their qualities, including scent. You could increase the range of fragrances changing the planting without altering the overall appearance.

Replace the passionflower and solanum with the equally attractive, sweetly scented *Jasminum officinale* f. *affine* and the unusual *Akebia quinata* (**pictured above**), which has more delicately fragrant, purple-chocolate flowers. Replace the upright yew with *Juniperus chinensis* 'Aurea', for its fragrant foliage and plant around it with bedding hyacinths 'Gipsy Queen'. For a dramatic feature replace the *Yucca filamentosa* 'Variegata' with *Y. whipplei*, which has a tall flowering stem covered with scented, greenish-white, purple-tinged flowers in late spring. In a cold winter this might need some protection.

You might change *Iris foetidissima* 'Variegata' for the sun-loving *I. graminea* and its purple scented flowers, and perhaps include the hardy pink-flowered *Chrysanthemum* 'Clara Curtis' instead of the cistus. Finally, as a replacement for the silver-blue *Festuca glauca* 'Blauglut', use the low-growing and long-flowering *Nepeta* × *faassenii* (catmint), with its grey-green leaves, or the dwarf blue lavender *Lavandula angustifolia* 'Hidcote', with its more rounded habit.

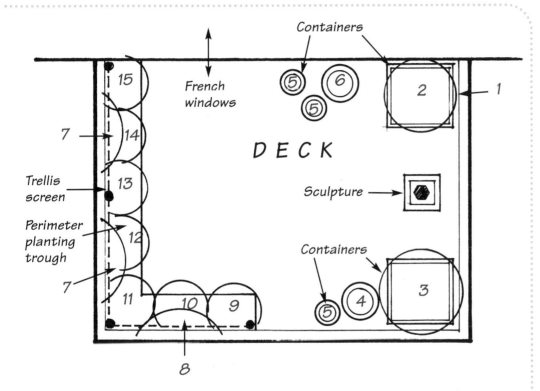

planting key

1 *Taxus baccata* 'Standishii'
2 *Tulipa* 'Peach Blossom'
3 *Elaeagnus pungens* 'Maculata'
4 *Cordyline australis* Purpurea Group
5 *Pelargonium zonale*
6 *Yucca filamentosa* 'Variegata'
7 *Passiflora caerulea*
8 *Solanum laxum* 'Album'
9 *Convolvulus cneorum*
10 *Lavandula* 'Helmsdale'
11 *Cistus* 'Silver Pink'
12 *Festuca glauca* 'Blauglut'
13 *Osteospermum ecklonis*
14 *Cytisus* × *kewensis*
15 *Iris foetidissima* 'Variegata'

• option 2

Shady Roof Garden

Shady roof gardens provide an opportunity to grow and display plants that benefit from a lack of direct sunlight, particularly if they can be sheltered from cold, dry winds.

Structure is created by large shrubs: the golden-leaved *Philadelphus coronarius* 'Aureus', which makes a bright focal point in one corner and has the bonus of white,

scented flowers and, opposite this, the variegated *Rhododendron ponticum* 'Variegatum', which produces large heads of purple trumpets in late spring.

There is plenty of colour on the trellis, provided by the large, pink-striped flowers of *Clematis* 'Nelly Moser' and the sweetly scented, reddish-purple blooms of the late-flowering *Lonicera periclymenum* 'Serotina' (late Dutch honeysuckle).

Shade-loving perennials provide splashes of both flower and foliage colour. The silver-leaved, trailing deadnettle *Lamium maculatum* 'Beacon Silver' has pink flowers; the deep glossy purple mounds of *Heuchera micrantha* var. *diversifolia* 'Palace Purple' are topped by tiny white flowers; and the leafy yet neat *Anemone hupehensis* var. *japonica* 'Bressingham Glow' has cheerful gold-centred, pink flowers.

Hardy ferns are excellent for shade, and *Dryopteris erythrosora* (buckler fern) is especially good, with glossy evergreen foliage and striking coppery-pink new growths. Spring-flowering bulbs are ideal for shady and woodland situations, and here large-flowered blue crocuses make an early bright patch of colour around the base of the philadelphus, which comes into leaf after the crocuses are finished, providing continuity.

plant group

CLIMBERS

Climbers are an indispensable group of garden plants. They can hide or screen unsightly objects or blank walls; they can be planted on or over arches, pergolas and gazebos to add valuable height and enhance the overall effect; and, depending on species, they can be used to grow up into and add interest to larger woody plants, such as trees and taller conifers.

They can be divided into two main types: those that produce aerial roots, such as *Hedera* species (ivy), which will adhere to almost any solid object, and those that need a structure, such as trellis, that they can twine their stems or clinging tendrils around, such as passionflower, *Passiflora caerulea* 'Constance Elliot' (**pictured above**) for example.

There is a climber for almost every garden situation. Perhaps the only place climbers will not thrive is in waterlogged, badly drained soil.

Flowers can range from the spectacular mauve racemes of *Wisteria sinensis* to the unusual, chocolately-purple pendents of *Akebia quinata* and the tiny but abundant and sweetly scented white flowers of *Clematis flammula*. Foliage form is equally varied, from the rough, pale yellow leaves of the golden hop, *Humulus lupulus* 'Aureus', to the pink, cream and green of *Actinidia kolomikta* .

Finally, scented climbers are a must for seating areas. *Jasminum* species (jasmine), climbing roses and, of course, *Lonicera* species (honeysuckle) are all excellent choice.

Containers

French windows

DECK

Sculpture →

Containers

Trellis screen

Perimeter planting trough

7

8

---

planting key

1 *Philadelphus coronarius* 'Aureus'
2 *Crocus* (large-flowered blue)
3 *Rhododendron ponticum* 'Variegatum'
4 *Aruncus dioicus*
5 *Impatiens* (red)
6 *Osmanthus heterophyllus* 'Variegatus'
7 *Clematis* 'Nelly Moser'
8 *Lonicera periclymenum* 'Serotina'

9 *Lamium maculatum* 'Beacon Silver'
10 *Aquilegia* McKana Group
11 *Heuchera micrantha* var. *diversifolia* 'Palace Purple'
12 *Luzula sylvatica* 'Aurea'
13 *Anemone hupehensis* var. *japonica* 'Bressingham Glow'
14 *Astilbe* 'Deutschland'
15 *Dryopteris erythrosora*

• option 3

Year-round Roof Garden

In small gardens, where it is only possible to grow a limited number of plants, it is essential that each of the plants you choose should give value for money either because it is evergreen or it has a long flowering period.

This roof garden design includes only 15 plants, but there is some interest almost all year round. Evergreens are essential in this type of garden. *Aucuba japonica* 'Crotonifolia' (spotted laurel) eventually makes a

substantial mound of large, gold-splashed leaves, ideal for sun or shade, while the neat mound of *Hebe* 'Red Edge', although attractive in summer with its white flowers, comes into its own in a hard winter, when the blue-green foliage becomes beautifully red-tinted. Equally striking and valuable for its permanent show is *Euonymus fortunei* 'Emerald 'n' Gold', which is a lovely contrast with the purple-red foliage of the dwarf *Berberis thunbergii* 'Atropurpurea Nana', which is also excellent value for its clusters of pinkish-cream flowers

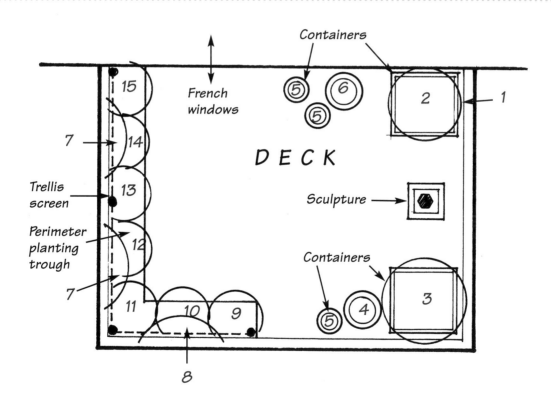

1 *Hydrangea macrophylla* 'Mariesii Perfecta'
2 *Galanthus nivalis*
3 *Aucuba japonica* 'Crotonifolia'
4 *Nerine bowdenii*
5 *Erica darleyensis* (mixed cultivars)
6 *Rhododendron* 'Praecox'
7 *Jasminum officinale* 'Aureum'
8 *Vitis vinifera* 'Purpurea'
9 *Genista lydia*
10 *Hebe* 'Red Edge'
11 *Aster novi-belgii* 'Little Pink Beauty'
12 *Berberis thunbergii* 'Atropurpurea Nana'
13 *Euonymus fortunei* 'Emerald 'n' Gold'
14 *Hemerocallis* 'Cherry Cheeks'
15 *Viburnum davidii*

in spring and brilliant orange-red autumn colour. Behind these, on the trellis, the same theme is continued with

the ornamental vine *Vitis vinifera* 'Purpurea', which has striking purple leaves, grapes and brilliant autumn colour, and *Jasminum officinale* 'Aureum', which has gold-splashed leaves and stems and produces scented white flowers in late summer.

The winter-flowering heather *Erica darleyensis*, growing in pots, makes cheerful spots of late colour, overlapping with the early spring delight of *Galanthus nivalis* (snowdrop), planted beneath the *Hydrangea macrophylla* 'Mariesii Perfecta'. The large blue mopheads of this appear in midsummer and are attractive for many weeks, even when the flowers have gone over.

Although the individual flowers of *Hemerocallis* 'Cherry Cheeks' only last a day or so, they are produced over a long period.

Plants for a Roof Garden

Roof gardens can be exposed to more wind and sun than an equivalent area at ground level. While you can improve these conditions to some degree with trellises and screens, in the long term careful plant selection will pay dividends. Wind-tolerant shrubs, particularly large evergreens such as elaeagnus, are essential for year-round colour and structure and their potential for creating some shelter. Many plants that do well in a coastal position – escallonia, fuchsia and cistus, for example – are ideal for hot, windy roof gardens. Grey- and silver-leaved plants, with leathery or soft, hairy leaves, are suitable for drier situations – *Artemisia* (mugwort), *Rosmarinus* (rosemary) and *Salvia officinalis* (sage), for example. Use tough-leaved climbers, such as *Hedera* species (ivy), and those with small leaves and wiry stems or with clusters of small flowers, such as *Jasminum officinale* and forms of *Lonicera*

periclymenum (common honeysuckle, woodbine). Plant low, short-stemmed bulbs, including *Galanthus* species (snowdrop, **pictured below**), crocus and species narcissus, and perennials with low, dense crowns and short-stemmed flowers, such as *Geranium renardii* and *Aster novi-belgii* 'Little Pink Beauty'.

plant group
CONIFERS

Many conifers make excellent garden plants, ranging in size from miniature dark green buns, like *Chamaecyparis obtusa* 'Nana', even suitable for a windowbox, right up to specimens of the Colorado spruce, such as *Picea pungens* 'Hoopsii', which makes a striking silver-blue cone to 15m (50ft) or more. The more compact and slow-growing types are ideal for a roof garden, providing year-round foliage interest.

There are many shades of green, some bright, as in the tall *Chamaecyparis lawsoniana* 'Green Hedger', some almost black, as in *Pinus heldreichii* 'Satellit'. There are many gold forms: the pale sulphur-yellow of the spreading *Juniperus* x *pfitzeriana* 'Sulphur', the bright gold of the neat, flame-shaped *Thuja orientalis* 'Aurea Nana' and the almost orange, winter tints of the feathery *Thuja occidentalis* 'Rheingold'.

Blue and silver types, like the tiny upright column of *Juniperus communis* 'Compressa', and the bright silver-blue tones of the blue *Picea* species (spruce) and *Abies* species (silver firs), are equally abundant. The low carpets of *Juniperus horizontalis* 'Hughes' and *J. horizontalis* 'Blue Chip' have purplish tints in cold winters.

Form and shape vary too. *Juniperus communis* 'Repanda' makes a prostrate mat, while *Chamaecyparis lawsoniana* 'Minima Glauca' is a neat globe. Fastigiate forms, such as *Pinus sylvestris* 'Fastigiata', make tall, narrow columns, while many spruces, including *Picea orientalis* 'Aurea', form the classic conical outlines.

Page numbers in *italic* refer to the images

a

Abelia x *grandiflora* 13
Abies 125
Abutilon 105
  A. milleri 105
  A. vitifolium 14, 15
Acaena saccaticupula 48
Acanthus 99
  A. mollis 29, 73, 98, 99
  A. spinosus 37
Acca selloviana 15
Acer grosseri 39, 107, *107*
  A. palmatum 39, 106–7, 108
  A. rufinerve 39
  A. shirasawanum 82–3
Achillea 29, 31, 74, 81
  A. lewisii 48, 49
  A. millefolium 81
acid soils 49
Aconitum 97
Acorus gramineus 13
Actinidia kolomikta 98, 99, 123
Adiantum pedatum 97
Adonis amurensis 25
Agapanthus 15, 29, 34, 4, 75, 89, 99
  A. campanulatus 55, 90, 91
Ajuga reptans 31, 32, 33, 47, 79, 116, 117
Akebia quinata 21, 121, *121*, 123
Alcea 75
  A. rosea 16, 74
Alchemilla 75
  A. alpina 47
  A. mollis 31, 72, 73, *73*
alkaline soils 13
Allium giganteum 32, 33
  A. roseum 32
  A. schoenoprasum 61
  A. schubertii 15, 37
  A. senescens 63
alpines 45, 47, 49, 110, 112–13
Ampelopsis glandulosa 41
Anacyclus pyrethrum 113
Anemone hupehensis 29, 87, 97, 123
  A. x *hybrida* 16, 21, 23, 71, 75, *75*
  A. sylvestris 24

annuals 104–5, 115
Anthemis punctata 79
Aquilegia 97, 123
  A. vulgaris 32, 74, 95
Arabis ferdinandicoburgi 45, 113
Aralia 99
  A. elata 15
Arenaria montana 47
Argyranthemum frutescens 105
Artemisia 25, 125
  A. alba 32, 63
  A. dracunculus 61
  A. ludoviciana 24
  A. 'Powis Castle' 16, 17, 21, 29, 55
  A. schmidtiana 47, 48–9, 49
  A. stelleriana 72, 73
Aruncus dioicus 16, 98, 123
Arundo donax 15
asparagus peas 64
Asphodeline lutea 15
Asplenium scolopendrium 73
Aster amellus 20, 21, 32, 33
  A. novae-angliae 23
  A. novi-belgii 24, 29, 49, 71, 87, 89, 124, 125
  A. thomsonii 74
Astericus 105
Astilbe 21, 29, 34, 47, 49, 71, 82, 83, 123
  A. x *arendsii* 16, 17, 56, 57, 74, 90, 95
Astilboides tabularis 38, 39
Athyrium niponicum 97
Aubrieta 47, 49
Aucuba japonica 82, 124
Aurinia saxatilis 81
Azalea 49
Azara microphylla 109

b

Ballota 32
  B. pseudodictamnus 13, *13*, 31
bamboos 99
beds and borders:
  corner beds 34–41
  island beds 26–33
  long, narrow borders 18–25
  planning 25
  rectangular borders 10–17
  single-colour

borders 24–5, 32–3, 49
beetroot 64, 65
Berberidopsis corallina 39, 87, 98
Berberis media 73
  B. x *ottawensis* 89, 95
  B. thunbergii 15, 28, 29, 30, 31, 32, 45, 57, 79, 81, 82, 90, 98, 99, 112, 113, 124–5
Bergenia 13, 25, 29, 31, 47
  B. cordifolia 95
berries 41
Betula utilis 107
Bidens ferulifolia 105, 115
Brachyscome 115
Buddleja 87, 91
bulbs 23, 41, 110
Buxus sempervirens 52–3, 57, 71, 107

c

Calamagrostis acutiflora 21
Calluna 49, 117
  C. vulgaris 13, 48, 71, 112, 113, 116, 117, *117*
Caltha palustris 97
Camellia 49, 91
  C. japonica 95
  C. x *williamsii* 38, 39
Campanula 81, 113
  C. alliariifolia 113
  C. carpatica 45, 48, 49, 113
  C. garganica 73
  C. glomerata 97, 113
  C. lactiflora 21, 29, 113
  C. latifolia 113
  C. persicifolia 16, 24, 75, 81
  C. portenschlagiana 113, *113*
  C. trachelium 113
Campsis x *tagliabuana* 14, 95
Carex morrowii 39
  C. oshimensis 31, 116, 117
Carpenteria californica 88, 89
Caryopteris 91
  C. clandonensis 79, 89
Ceanothus 88, 89, 91, *91*
  C. dentatus 94, 95
  C. thyrsiflorus 89
Centaurea macrocephala 23
Centranthus 75
  C. ruber 23

Cephalaria alpina 113
Cerastium tomentosum 81
Ceratostigma 91
  C. plumbaginoides 79
  C. willmottianum 74, 75
Cercis siliquastrum 37
Chamaecyparis lawsoniana 44, 45,48, 57, 125
  C. obtusa 125
  C. pisifera 98, 99
Chimonanthus praecox 109
Choisya 82
  C. ternata 71, *71*, 87, 89, 96, 97
Chrysanthemum 40, 121
Cimicifuga simplex 31
Cistus 13, 121, 125
  C. x *hybridus* 36, 37
Clematis 75
  C. alpina 81, 82, 89
  C. armandii 12, 13
  C. 'Barbara Jackman' 94, 95
  C. cirrhosa 17, 90
  C. flammula 39, 123
  C. florida 89
  C. 'Henryi' 24, 25
  C. 'Lincoln Star' 96, 97
  C. montana 40
  C. 'Nelly Moser' 21, 21, 82, 122, 123
  C. 'Royal Velours' 89
  C. 'Ville de Lyon' 90
  C. 'Vyvyan Pennell' 21
climbers 123
Colchicum 23
colour 117
  containers 104–5
  'cool' colour schemes 80–1
  cottage gardens 75, 95
  formal gardens 54–5
  patio gardens 88–9
  raised beds 48–9
  single-colour borders 24–5, 32–3, 49
  stems 107
conifers 47, 49, 110, 125
containers 100–17
Convolvulus cneorum 79, 121
Cordyline australis 13, 121
Coreopsis verticillata

23, 87
corner beds 34–41
Cornus 15, 91
  C. alba 31, 39, 90, 91, 107
  C. canadensis 91, 91, 97
  C. controversa 31
  C. kousa 91
  C. mas 91
  C. sanguinea 91, 107
Corydalis flexuosa 47
Corylus maxima 14–15, 98
Cotinus coggygria 31, 73
Cotoneaster 41
  C. atropurpureus 73, 87
  C. congestus 45
  C. dammeri 79
  C. frigidus 41, *41*
  C. simonsii 40, 41
cottage-garden style 20–1, 74–5, 94–5
courtyard gardens 92–9
crabapples 64
Crambe cordifolia 24
Crepis incana 48, 49
Crinodendron hookerianum 15
Crinum powellii 109
Crocosmia 21, 29, 81, *81*, 89
  C. x *crocosmiiflora* 16, 74, 75
Crocus 107, 110, 123, 125
  C. chrysanthus 23
  C. tommasinianus 23, *23*
x *Cupressocyparis leylandii* 57
Cyclamen coum 23
Cytisus x *kewensis* 121

d

Daboecia 117
Daphne cneorum 37
Decaisnea fargesii 15, 41
Delphinium 16, 21, 24, 25, 95
  D. grandiflorum 48, 49
Dianthus 'Arctic Star' 104, 105
  D. 'Devon Glow' 95
  D. 'Devon Maid' 21
  D. 'Diane' 95
  D. 'Doris' 29, 90, 91
  D. 'Garland' 45
  D. 'Pike's Pink' 113
Diascia 105, 115
  D. barberae 48, 49

Dicentra 29, 32, 74, 75
  D. formosa 82, 83
Digitalis 21, 75
  D. lutea 97
  D. purpurea 23, 24
Doronicum 29
dry gardens 13, 78–9, 120–1
Dryopteris erythrosora 31, 97, 123
  D. filix-mas 97

e

Echinacea purpurea 95
Echinops ritro 23
Elaeagnus 125
  E. ebbingei 57
  E. pungens 13, 47, 79, 90, 98, 120, 121
Enkianthus campanulatus 39
Epilobium glabellum 45, 47
Epimedium x *perralchicum* 47
  E. rubrum 97
Eranthis hyemalis 23
Erica 49, 117
  E. arborea 117
  E. carnea 13, 45, 89, 107, 116, 117
  E. darleyensis 71, 87, 116, 117, 124, 125
  E. erigena 40, 41, 117
  E. vagans 13, 47, 71, 117
ericaceous plants 13, 49
Eryngium agavifolium 23
  E. bourgatii 55, 90–1
  E. variifolium 31
Erythronium 97
Escallonia 125
Euonymus fortunei 13, 56, 57, 87, 90, 116, 124
Euphorbia 25
  E. amygdaloides 71
  E. characias 23, 79
  E. griffithii 15, 74
  E. polychroma 20, 21, 29
  E. wallichii 16, 17
evergreens 12–13, 70
exotic flowers 14–15

f

Fagus sylvatica 57
Fargesia murieliae 13, 31, 99

F. nitida 31, *31*, 99
Fatsia japonica 98
Felicia amelloides 115
fennel, Florence 64, 65
ferns 97
Festuca glauca 13, 31, 32, 33, *33*, 45, 121
  F. valesiaca 108, 109
Filipendula ulmaria 38, 39, 87
flower arranger's garden 28–9
focal points 33
Foeniculum vulgare 23, 37, 87
foliage: containers 108–9
formal beds 52–3
front gardens 72–3
island beds 30–1
formal beds 50–7
Forsythia 91
Fragaria ananassa 65, 65
French beans 64, 65
front gardens 68–75
Fuchsia 125
  F. 'Annabel' 105
  F. 'Genii' 107
  F. 'Lady in Pink' 114, 115
  F. 'Lady Thumb' 79
  F. 'Marinka' 105
  F. 'Mrs Popple' 57

g

Galanthus 45, 110, 125, *125*
  G. nivalis 23, 124, 125
Galtonia candicans 40, 41
Gaultheria mucronata 41
Genista hispanica 37
  G. lydia 79, 124
  G. pilosa 81
Geranium 83
  G. cinereum 45
  G. clarkei 21
  G. himalayense 29
  G. ibericum 83, 89, 99
  G. x *lindavicum* 83
  G. macrorrhizum 17, 21, 83
  G. x *oxonianum* 74, 75, 83
  G. phaeum 75, 82, 83, 87, 99
  G. psilostemon 83, *83*
  G. renardii 31, 83, 125
  G. sanguineum 16, 17

G. sylvaticum 75
G. wallichianum 49
Geum 95
G. rivale 82
grasses 33
gravel gardens 86–7
groundcover plants 47
Gypsophila repens 79

• **h**

Hakonechloa macra 39, 39
Hamamelis 91
H. x intermedia 17
hanging baskets 110
heathers 47, 49, 70–1, 110, 117
Hebe armstrongii 15
H. 'Bowles's Hybrid' 81
H. 'Great Orme' 13
H. 'Margret' 23
H. 'Marjorie' 79
H. ochracea 46, 47
H. pimeleoides 23, 48, 49
H. pinguifolia 15
H. 'Red Edge' 17, 124
H. 'White Gem' 13
H. 'Wingletye' 40
H. 'Youngii' 45
Hedera 47, 123, 125
H. colchica 13, 17, 23, 41
H. helix 47, 79, 81, 87, 89, 96, 97, 108, 109, 116
hedges 57
Helianthemum 'The Bride' 37
H. 'Henfield Brilliant' 49, 78–9
H. 'Old Gold' 49
H. 'Rhodanthe Carneum' 13
H. 'Wisley Primrose' 45, 48
H. 'Wisley White' 48
Helic Hrysum petiolare 105, 115
Helictotrichon sempervirens 81
Heliotropium 105
Helleborus argutifolius 13, 31, 90
H. niger 24, 29
Hemerocallis 99
H. 'Burning Daylight' 71
H. 'Cherry Cheeks' 81, 124, 125
H. citrina 81

H. 'Hyperion' 89
herbaceous borders 16–17
herbs 37, 60–3, 110
Heuchera 73
H. micrantha 25, 31, 53, 53, 97, 123
H. 'Pewter Moon' 47
H. 'Rachel' 32, 71, 81
Heucherella tiarelloides 82
Holcus mollis 24
Hosta 25, 34, 47, 47, 49, 99
H. 'August Moon' 29
H. 'Big Daddy' 98
H. fortunei 72, 73
H. 'Frances Williams' 21, 29, 39
H. 'Gold Standard' 97
H. 'Halcyon' 21, 31, 39
H. 'Honeybells' 109
H. 'Krossa Regal' 53
H. plantaginea 87
H. 'Royal Standard' 89
H. sieboldiana 81
H. undulata 81
H. 'Wide Brim' 82
hot, dry gardens 78–9, 120–1
Houttuynia cordata 29, 29, 41
Humulus lupulus 123
Hyacinthoides nonscripta 87
Hyacinthus 121
Hydrangea 75, 91
H. anomala 90
H. arborescens 71
H. aspera 75, 87, 95
H. macrophylla 15, 87, 124, 125
H. paniculata 91
H. quercifolia 82, 83
H. serrata 39, 97
Hypericum 71
H. moserianum 90
Hyssopus officinalis 61

• **i**

Ilex 15
I. aquifolium 12, 13, 28, 29, 57, 70, 71, 73
I. crenata 13, 89
Impatiens 105, 115, 115, 123

Imperata cylindrica 15
Iris 25
I. 'Amber Queen' 48
I. 'Berkeley Gold' 81
I. 'Blue Pigmy' 32, 33
I. 'Braithwaite' 20, 21
I. 'Butterscotch Kiss' 95
I. 'Dancers Veil' 15
I. danfordiae 45
I. foetidissima 29, 31, 41, 75, 97, 121
I. 'Frost and Flame' 79
I. graminea 87, 121
I. 'Green Spot' 32, 33
I. pallida 72–3, 81
I. reticulata 45
I. sibirica 29, 97
I. 'Tinkerbell' 49
I. unguicularis 25, 29
I. 'White City' 24
island beds 10, 26–33

• **j**

Jasminum 34, 109, 123
J. nudiflorum 74, 89, 97
J. officinale 79, 87, 90, 91, 95, 109, 109, 121, 124, 125
J. stephanense 24, 25
Juniperus 47
J. chinensis 121
J. communis 44, 45, 57, 112, 113, 125
J. horizontalis 70, 71, 79, 125
J. x pfitzeriana 31, 45, 47, 87, 125
J. sabina 81

• **k**

Kirengeshoma palmata 39
kitchen gardens 58–65
Kniphofia 24, 25, 75
K. uvaria 16
Koelreuteria paniculata 73

M. lomariifolia 15, 31
M. x media 15, 15, 31
Malus 71
M. hupehensis 75
M. robusta 41
M. zumi 41
Matteuccia struthiopteris 71, 97, 97
Mediterranean beds 36–7
Melissa officinalis 31, 61, 61, 63, 82, 97
Mentha x gentilis 63
M. spicata 61
minimalist gardens 98–9
Miscanthus 99
M. sinensis 23, 24, 25, 71, 73, 89
moist, shady beds 38–9
Monarda 23, 95

• **n**

Nandina domestica 98
Narcissus 125
N. bulbocodium 23
N. 'Canaliculatus' 23
N. 'February Gold' 23
N. 'January Gold' 23
Nemesia caerulea 104, 105
Nepeta x faassenii 23, 29, 63, 121
Nerine bowdenii 124

• **o**

Ocimum basilicum 61
Oenothera macrocarpa 89
Ophiopogon planiscapus 31, 32, 47, 108–9, 109
Origanum vulgare 23, 40, 53, 61, 63
Osmanthus 109
O. x burkwoodii 40, 57
O. heterophyllus 123
Osmunda regalis 97
Osteospermum ecklonis 78, 79, 121

• **m**

Magnolia stellata 74
Mahonia 91, 99, 109
M. aquifolium 87

• **p**

Pachysandra 47
P. terminalis 40

Paeonia lactiflora 74, 75, 87
Panicum virgatum 71
Papaver orientale 74, 89, 95, 95
Parahebe lyallii 46, 47
Passiflora 34
P. caerulea 121, 123, 123
patio gardens 84–91
paving 75
Pelargonium 105, 115
P. zonale 121
Penstemon 89
P. newberryi 15
P. pinifolius 49
peonies 25
perennials 17, 25
Perovskia 71, 90, 91
Persicaria affinis 23, 87
P. vacciniifolia 45
Petroselinum crispum 61, 62
Petunia 105, 115
Philadelphus 25, 74, 75, 87, 109
P. coronarius 122, 123
Phlox carolina 95
P. maculata 16, 75
P. paniculata 21, 24, 29, 74, 95
P. subulata 48, 49, 81
Phormium 15, 30, 31, 108
P. tenax 13, 73
Photinia x fraseri 13, 15, 73
Phygelius rectus 15
Phyllostachys aurea 99
P. aureosulcata 98, 99
Physocarpus opulifolius 73, 89
Picea 125
P. orientalis 125
P. pungens 125
Pieris formosa 13
P. japonica 82
pink borders 32–3
Pinus heldreichii 125
P. sylvestris 125
Pittosporum 73
P. tenuifolium 81
planting perennials 17
Platycodon grandiflorus 15, 24, 32
Polygonatum x hybridum 82, 83
P. multiflorum 90
P. odoratum 97
Polystichum polyblepharum 82, 97
Potentilla 95
P. fruticosa 71, 81

P. recta 95
Primula denticulata 16, 82, 83, 83
P. japonica 39
pruning shrubs 91
Prunus laurocerasus 15, 71
P. serrula 107
Pulmonaria 24, 47
P. longifolia 47
P. saccharata 21
Pulsatilla vulgaris 45, 48, 49
purple borders 32–3
Pyracantha 41, 86–7

• **r**

raised beds 42–9, 78
rectangular borders 10–17
Rheum 98, 99
Rhodanthemum hosmariense 45
Rhododendron 47, 49
R. 'Alice' 39
R. 'Blue Danube' 49
R. 'Chikor' 46, 47
R. Gertrud Schäle Group 89
R. 'Gibraltar' 40, 41, 97
R. luteum 87
R. 'Mother of Pearl' 12, 13
R. 'Palestrina' 32, 48
R. ponticum 122, 123
R. 'Praecox' 124
R. 'Vuyk's Rosyred' 82
Ribes viburnifolium 13, 87
Rodgersia aesculifolia 72, 73
R. pinnata 89
roof gardens 118–25
Rosa 109
R. 'Albertine' 16, 21
R. 'Bonica' 40, 41, 41
R. 'Buff Beauty' 74, 75
R. 'Climbing Iceberg' 88, 89
R. 'Geranium' 41, 87
R. 'Golden Showers' 88, 89
R. 'Graham Thomas' 74, 75
R. 'Madame Alfred Carrière' 24, 25, 25
R. 'Nozomi' 79
R. 'Paul's Lemon Pillar' 81

R. 'Paul's Scarlet Climber' 81, 95
R. 'Pink Grootendorst' 57
R. rugosa 'Alba' 95
R. 'Schoolgirl' 90, 91
R. 'Zéphirine Drouhin' 87, 95
Roscoea cautleyoides 15
Rosmarinus 37, 125
R. officinalis 36–7, 60, 61
Rubus henryi 97
R. thibetanus 107
ruby chard 64, 65
Rudbeckia 16, 21
R. fulgida 81, 89, 89

• **s**

sage 37, 37
Salix 15, 107
S. alba 107
S. daphnoides 107
S. integra 108
S. lanata 73
Salvia 115
S. nemorosa 16, 95
S. officinalis 37, 61, 62, 63, 125
S. x sylvestris 21, 40, 41
Santolina chamaecyparissus 89
Sarcococca confusa 87
S. hookeriana 13
Sasa tsuboiana 13
Scabiosa 21
S. caucasica 24, 95
scented flowers 74–5, 109, 121
Schizophragma hydrangeoides 95
Schizostylis coccinea 25, 25, 90
Sedum 16, 17, 45
S. aizoon 21
S. spathulifolium 116–17
S. spectabile 23, 29
S. telephium 33, 40
Sempervivum 45, 116, 117
shade 83
cottage gardens 21
courtyard gardens 96–7
flower arranger's garden 29
formal gardens 56–7
gravel gardens 87
moist, shady beds 38–9
roof gardens 122–3
terraces 82–3

shrubs 15
  pruning 91
Sisyrinchium
  idahoense 49
Skimmia japonica
  23, 87, 116,
  117, *117*
  S. laureola 39
sloping gardens
  76–83
Solanum laxum 23,
  121
Solidago 16, 90
Sorbus 41
  S. hupehensis 40,
  41
  S. koehneana 89
Spartium junceum
  37
Spiraea 74
  S. betulifolia 24
  S. japonica 28, 29,
  73, 90
  S. nipponica 89
spring onions 64,
  65
Stachys byzantina
  30–1, 32, 37
stems, colourful
  107
Stipa 33, 99
  S. arundinacea 79,
  98
  S. calamagrostis
  23, 90, 91
  S. gigantea 21
strawberries 64,
  65, 65
sunny sites 39

Sutera cordata 115
Symphoricarpos
  doorenbosii 97
Symphytum 23, 47
Syringa 75
  S. meyeri 74

● t

Tagetes 115
Tanacetum
  parthenium 63
Taxus baccata 31,
  56–7, 73, 82, 87,
  120, 121
Tellima grandiflora
  90
terraces 78, 80–1,
  82–3
Teucrium
  chamaedrys 79
  T. fruticans 81
Thalictrum flavum
  16
Thuja occidentalis
  44, 45, 71, 125
  T. orientalis 57,
  125
Thunbergia alata
  114, 115
Thymus doefleri 113
  T. pulegioides 47,
  49
  T. serpyllum 37, 109
  T. vulgaris 61, 63
Tiarella cordifolia
  56, 57

Tilia 109
tomatoes 64, 65
Trachelospermum
  jasminoides 37
Tradescantia x
  andersoniana 16,
  21, 24, 32
Trifolium repens 32
Tsuga canadensis
  45, 47, 81
Tulipa 121

● u

Uncinia rubra 33

● v

Vaccinium
  vitisidaea 38, 39
vegetables 64–5
Verbascum 21, 75,
  95
  V. chaixii 24
Verbena 105
Veronica
  peduncularis 107
  V. prostrata 49
  V. spicata 48, 49,
  81
Viburnum 25, 109
  V. x *bodnantense*
  17, 91
  V. daVidii 30, 31,
  73, 124
  V. farreri 15

V. opulus 15, 87
V. tinus 41, 47, 70,
  71, 81, 90, 91
Vinca 47
  V. minor 25, 81,
  82, 108, 109
Viola 21, 40, 47,
  48, 107, 113
  V. odorata 41, 63
  V. riviniana 32, 81
Vitis coignetiae 31,
  98
  V. vinifera 37, 124,
  125

● w

Weigela 31, 91
  W. florida 74, 90
white borders 24–5
wildlife 22–3, 40–1
windowboxes
  110–17
windy sites 125
Wisteria 54, 55
  W. sinensis 123

● y

year-round interest
  17, 23, 44–5,
  90–1, 106–7,
  124–5
Yucca filamentosa
  121

Y. gloriosa 79, 79
Y. whipplei 121

● z

Zantedeschia
  aethiopica 15

● acknowledgements

Executive Editor Emily Van Eesteren

Editor Abi Rowsell

Senior Designer Joanna Bennett

Designer Tony Cohen

Senior Production Controller Louise Hall

Picture Researcher Christine Junemann

Colour illustrations Gill Tomblin

Black & white illustrations Tim Newbury

Photography:
Mark Bolton 99 top left, 107
  Corbis UK Ltd/Eric Chrichton 125 top left
Garden Picture Library The Old Vicarage,
  East Ruston, Norfolk, des; Graham
  Robson & Alan Gray 66–67
  Mark Bolton 89

David Cavagnaro 115
John Glover 5 left, 33 top right, 41 top
left, 65 top left, 83 top left
Neil Holmes 75 top right
Tim Macmillan 25 bottom centre
John Miller 50–51
Jerry Pavia 31
Howard Rice 49 top right, 55, 87,
125 Bottom
JS Sira 8–9, 13, 18–19, 58–59, 76–77,
91 top right
Friedrich Strauss 109 top right
Brigitte Thomas 57 bottom centre
Juliette Wade 63, 83 Bottom
Steve Wooster 100–101
John Glover 41 top left, 65 top left,
83 top left
Jerry Harpur/Des; Carol Rosenberg 33 top
left, 33 bottom centre, 37, 44, 49 bottom
centre, 65 top right, 84–85, 92–93, 99
top right, 105, 109 bottom, 117 top right,

118–119, 121, 123, 125 top right
Marcus Harpur 15, 17 top left, 41 top
right, 97, 102–103
Andrew Lawson 1, 5 centre right, 17 top
right, 21, 23, 29, 34–35, 42–43, 49 top
left, 73, 81, 83 top right, 91 Bottom,
110–111, 117 bottom
Octopus Publishing Group Limited/Mark
Bolton 109 top left
S & O Mathews 25 top right, 26–27, 41
bottom centre, 47, 53, 57 top left, 70, 91
top left, 95, 113
Clive Nichols Photography/Sir Terence
Conran 5 centre left, 10–11, 17 bottom
centre, 39, 57 top right, 61, 65 bottom
centre, 68–69, 75 top left, 75 bottom,
79, 117 top left
Jerry Pavia 25 top left
Jason Smalley 5 right
Rob Whitworth/Design; Beth Chatto 2–3,
99 Bottom